I0113248

Free Speech and Campus Civility

Free Speech and Campus Civility

Promoting Challenging but Constructive Dialog in Higher Education

Jeffrey L. Buller and Robert E. Cipriano

Foreword by Charles J. Russo

ROWMAN & LITTLEFIELD
Lanham • Boulder • New York • London

Published by Rowman & Littlefield
A wholly owned subsidiary of The Rowman & Littlefield Publishing Group, Inc.
4501 Forbes Boulevard, Suite 200, Lanham, Maryland 20706
www.rowman.com

6 Tinworth Street, London SE11 5AL, United Kingdom

Copyright © 2021 by Jeffrey L. Buller and Robert E. Cipriano

All rights reserved. No part of this book may be reproduced in any form or by any electronic or mechanical means, including information storage and retrieval systems, without written permission from the publisher, except by a reviewer who may quote passages in a review.

British Library Cataloguing in Publication Information Available

Library of Congress Cataloging-in-Publication Data

Names: Buller, Jeffrey L., author. | Cipriano, Robert E., 1945– author. | Russo, Charles J., writer of foreword.
Title: Free speech and campus civility : promoting challenging but constructive dialog in higher education / Jeffrey L. Buller and Robert E. Cipriano ; foreword by Charles J. Russo.
Description: Lanham : Rowman & Littlefield, [2021] | Includes bibliographical references and index.
Identifiers: LCCN 2021005825 (print) | LCCN 2021005826 (ebook) | ISBN 9781475861341 (cloth) | ISBN 9781475861358 (paperback) | ISBN 9781475861365 (ebook)
Subjects: LCSH: Academic freedom—United States. | Freedom of speech—United States. | Education, Higher—Moral and ethical aspects—United States.
Classification: LCC LC72.2 .B85 2021 (print) | LCC LC72.2 (ebook) | DDC 378.1/21—dc23
LC record available at https://lccn.loc.gov/2021005825
LC ebook record available at https://lccn.loc.gov/2021005826

For our wives, Sandra and Raffaela, as well as all the brave essential workers and first responders who served others selflessly during the COVID-19 pandemic.

Contents

Foreword

As Jeffrey L. Buller and Robert E. Cipriano presciently illustrate in this very readable volume, *Free Speech and Campus Civility: Promoting Challenging but Constructive Dialogue in Higher Education*, the present "is a time of unprecedented change in higher education" not just in the United States, the focus of this engaging book, but throughout the world. Institutions of higher education face two different, yet equally real and dangerous, types of threats, external and internal, during this unprecedented, challenging time.

Externally, the impact of the COVID-19 pandemic threatens the existential viability not just of smaller institutions but also of larger colleges and universities. This threat emerges as the shift to virtual learning via Zoom and other such platforms have demonstrated that the traditional "chalk and talk" approach of rote learning in lecture halls seems to be going the way of the dinosaur. Moreover, parents are increasingly reluctant to spend exorbitant sums to send their children to colleges and universities where their offspring often come home espousing ideals rebuffing the very values they learned growing up. At the same time, students appear to be unwilling to incur crushing debt to be educated by passively sitting in their dormitories or off-campus housing in front of their computer screens or other devices as their instructors drone on in their lectures.

The internal threats facing colleges and universities at the heart of this volume may well be even more insidious than the external dangers because they attack the very heart of what it means to be stakeholders in higher education. More specifically, increasing numbers of faculty members have eschewed teaching, scholarship, and academic freedom essentially to become activists whose aims are to indoctrinate, rather than instruct, their students into espousing the perspectives of the politically correct flavors of the day. Such "teaching" has negatively impacted genuine learning as institutions that once served as safe harbors open to the free and robust exchange of ideas without repercussion have become the antithesis of these ideals.

Further exacerbating the status of free speech, as Buller and Cipriano accurately portray it, too many faculty members and administrators in growing numbers of colleges and universities have, either intentionally or because of their failure to intervene, seen increasing percentages of those on their campuses reject the cherished ideal of having their institutions serve as part of the marketplace of ideas. In these cherished spaces, students, faculty members, and others were free, even encouraged, to engage in vociferous exchanges in which they could disagree with one another, often boisterously so, without becoming personally disagreeable. Sadly, such exchanges are uncommon today.

At the same time, just as many faculty members demonstrate their intolerance by brooking no dissent from students, colleagues, or others who dissent from their politically correct rantings of the day that are supposed to pass as "teaching," experiences imposed on both of my own children, who escaped unscathed, during their undergraduate educations, the nature of free speech on campuses has been altered radically. As many leaders of the free speech movement of the 1960s described in the second chapter of this thought-provoking volume have come to occupy positions of leadership on campuses, including faculty hiring committees, they have taught their students to be increasingly hostile to ideas with which they disagree.

One has only to peruse newspaper headlines in recent years to learn of the incivility, intolerance, disrespect, and violence students have increasingly directed at speakers with whom they disagreed. Among the speakers who have been shouted down, or "cancelled," as it is now called, or disinvited to campuses are conservative pundit Milo Yiannopoulos, International Monetary Fund chief Christine Lagarde, former secretary of state Condoleezza Rice, sociologist Charles Murray, Somali refugee and activist Ayaan Hirsi Ali, and conservative commentator Ben Shapiro to name but a few.

Along with growing intolerance of views to which they do not agree, other than at a few bastions of traditional liberal learning as exemplified by the University of Chicago, campus officials have had to issue "trigger warnings" and create "safe spaces" for students who respond as frightened children rather than adults on encountering views inconsistent with their own. *Trigger warnings* is a term of art borrowed from the literature on mental health associated with the diagnosis of posttraumatic stress syndrome. Warnings can be verbal, written, or virtual, as in online, is to inform students they may be exposed to or harmed by potentially traumatic material with which they might disagree or find offensive. Safe spaces are locations on campuses, whether residence halls or other designated areas, where students can gather to avoid exposure to ideas with which they disagree or to discuss their reactions to ideas they consider offensive.

In what may be an extreme, a safe space at Brown University "included cookies, coloring books, bubbles, Play-Doh, calming music, pillows, blankets, a video of playful puppies and trained professionals to deal with the traumatized." Campus officials at Brown created the safe space in response to student need following an on-campus debate over whether a rape culture exists in the United States. As officials at American colleges and universities coddle students who demand protection from ideas with which they disagree, rather than bullets, one can only wonder where the safe spaces were for the eighteen- to twenty-one-year-olds, the same age as today's campus populations, who assaulted Normandy Beach on D-Day.

Against the preceding background, Buller and Cipriano examine the status of free speech on campuses by exploring ways in which leaders in today's institutions, even with the shifting mores of the day, must act to protect what may be the most precious of American rights. After detailing how civility in free speech on campuses has become something of an endangered, almost anachronistic, ideal, the authors offer practical suggestions for preserving both free speech and civility on campuses. Buller and Cipriano handily accomplish their goal in a highly readable format by, for example, suggesting that campus leaders use incidents wherein free speech is threatened or endangered as teachable moments to explain the inestimable value of civil discourse in our free, open American society and by encouraging faculty members in all disciplines, as appropriate, to assist students, and others, on campuses to work together to value the free, open, and civil exchange of ideas on America campuses and beyond.

Keeping in mind Heraclitus's often-stated dictum that "one cannot step into the same river twice" because the flowing water continually makes it new, the same can be said about the endangered status of civility and free speech on American campuses. More specifically, in light of how rapidly attitudes on campuses have changed in recent years, the words of a federal trial court in Missouri are instructive: "It is unpopular speech which needs the protection of the First Amendment. The First Amendment was designed for this very purpose" (*Beussink ex rel. Beussink v. Woodland R-IV School District*, 30 F.Supp.2d 1175, 1182 [E.D. Mo. 1998]).

As debate about free speech in American higher education rages on, *Free Speech and Campus Civility* is destined to serve as a greatly welcomed, valuable addition to the professional library of administrators, faculty members, students, and all interested in safeguarding the free exchange of ideas in colleges and universities even, or maybe especially, those that may be unpopular. Readers will happily accept the challenge of heeding the call of Buller and

Cipriano to protect free speech and civility on campuses because in so doing they will help to ensure high-quality, open-minded educational experiences for students and others affiliated with American colleges and universities.

Charles J. Russo, JD, EdD
Panzer Chair in Education
Research Professor of Law
University of Dayton, Ohio

Preface

The observation that "this is a time of unprecedented change in higher education" has become overused to the point of being rendered meaningless. The Morrill Acts of 1862 and 1890 that led to the creation of land-grant universities in the United States brought about a time of unprecedented change. The GI Bill of 1944 that enabled thousands of American military veterans to attend college at little or no cost brought about a time of unprecedented change.

The desegregation of American universities in the 1950s and 1960s brought about a time of unprecedented change. It is the nature of higher education in the modern world to change as society changes, and any innovation that fundamentally changes the context in which students learn and faculty members teach or conduct research may be described as "unprecedented."

And yet the first quarter of the twenty-first century has brought about so many unexpected developments that it does seem fair to say, "This is a time of unprecedented change in higher education." At public institutions, the percentage of an institution's budget that is funded by the state has continued to decline. Tuition rates have thus increased, with the result that students are increasingly graduating with an almost unbearable amount of student debt.

Legislatures and governing boards have taken more activist positions about what should and should not be covered in the classroom. The result has been, as we'll explore in the last chapter of this book, a new intensity in discussions about the very purpose of college, leaving many potential students and their parents wondering whether higher education is worth the investment of time and money that it requires.

As though all these factors were not enough, the global pandemic of 2020 caused universities all over the world to suspend their classes or convert courses from traditional to online formats. Once many classrooms became virtual, it seemed fair to wonder whether the time-honored custom of professors and students meeting face to face would ever return.

Parents and students, who were angry enough about the high cost of college, became even angrier when they saw classroom experiences replaced by video conferences. Faculty members, who were already angry about budget cuts, became even angrier about the constant demands that they do more and more with less and less.

Administrators, who were already angry about the degree to which legislatures and governing boards told them how to do their jobs, became even angrier as they found themselves caught in the middle between competing mandates for public safety and personalized education. Debates that were once (relatively) civil turned into firestorms as free speech was seen as entitling people to shout their opinions, whether informed or not, into the faces of others and as protests sometimes turned into riots.

This book is an attempt to explore whether it is even possible in these difficult times to protect free speech while promoting campus civility. We'll explore some of the history that has brought higher education to its current point and examine what several institutions have done to carve out a middle path that allows both free speech and civility to thrive.

Through this middle path, we hope that readers will challenge their own beliefs about the nature and limits of free speech and about the way in which civil discourse is either essential or irrelevant to the goals of higher education. For campuses that are struggling with challenges to free speech, campus civility, or both, we hope to offer some practical solutions about what works so that schools can learn from the successes of others and avoid their mistakes.

This is a time of unprecedented change in higher education.

Introduction

Every organizational challenge has its context. It can be impossible to reverse a budgetary decline unless you know the financial problems or patterns of expenditures that caused it. It can be impossible to decrease unsustainable rates of student attrition unless you know why students are failing to persist. And it can be impossible to protect both free speech and civility on campus without understanding why they have so often come to be in conflict.

Free Speech and Campus Civility: Promoting Challenging but Constructive Dialogue in Higher Education thus begins with an overview of why many professors and administrators believe that there is a problem in higher education today. We examine several events that appear to indicate conflicts between the right of free speech and the desirability of campus civility, and we trace some of the most immediate causes of this apparent conflict.

Next we offer examples of three practical approaches that colleges and universities of various sizes and missions have attempted to implement as ways of seeking a balance between unrestricted free speech and a level of civility that allows for rational discourse without descending into artificial politeness for the sake of politeness or an overly restrictive "political correctness." We consider what worked, what didn't work, and what made various approaches either sustainable or merely temporary.

The intended audience for *Free Speech and Campus Civility* is anyone who works in or cares about higher education. Faculty members and administrators will find it particularly useful either for individual study or as part of a professional development program. Institutions in crisis can use it to learn about potential ways to mitigate their current problems. Courses in higher education leadership might adopt it as a textbook. And student government personnel will find it a valuable source of ideas for co-curricular and extra-curricular activities.

The book grew out of a webinar that the authors developed as a way of providing guidance to institutions that were struggling from campus protests that began peacefully but sometimes devolved into violence or claims of free speech that were used to silence the speech of others. It was then expanded by studies of additional examples of how campus disruptions were addressed, interviews with people responsible for promoting campus programs on free speech and civility, and research based in the fields of conflict resolution and nonviolent confrontation.

We'd like to thank Jon Crylen and *The Academic Leader* for permission to reprint the case study included in Chapter 2. This case study first appeared in Cipriano, R. E, & Buller, J. L. (2020, March 16). Campus incivility and free speech: A contemporary dilemma. *Academic Leader*. https://www.academic-leader.com/topics/institutional-culture/campus-incivility-and-free-speech-a-contemporary-dilemma.

We'd also like to thank our editor at Rowman and Littlefield, Tom Koerner, for his consistent support throughout this and many other projects; Sandra McClain for editorial and research assistance; and all those institutions mentioned in the pages that follow for providing excellent examples for the rest of us to follow.

Jeffrey L. Buller
Raleigh, North Carolina

Robert E. Cipriano
Madison, Connecticut
October 1, 2020

Chapter One

The Conflict of Free Speech and Campus Civility

In the fall of 2019, faculty members at Georgia Southern University, a large regional university located in the small town of Statesboro, located about fifty-five miles west of Savannah, had assigned all first-year students to read the same book. The idea of this "common reading program," popular at many colleges and universities, was to provide incoming students with a shared intellectual experience and help build community. The result was exactly the opposite.

The book chosen as that year's common reader was Jennine Capó Crucet's *Make Your Home among Strangers* (2016), a novel about a Cuban immigrant who leaves home to go to college in the midst of family turmoil. Professors at Georgia Southern hoped that students would relate to the characters in the novel, better appreciate the challenges faced by minorities (the school's student population is roughly two-thirds white and one-third minority), and have an opportunity to speak about the issue of how the United States should deal with undocumented workers, a significant national issue at the time.

As a way of advancing these goals, Capó Crucet was invited to campus to speak to students about her book. During one of these public events, she read part of an essay from one of her other books, *My Time among the Whites* (2019). A number of students were offended by the title of this work, which they regarded as racist, and the tone of Capó Crucet's essay.

During the question and answer session, one student observed the following. "I noticed that you made a lot of generalizations about the majority of white people being privileged. What makes you believe that it's okay to come to a college campus like this, when we are supposed to be promoting diversity on this campus, which is what we're taught? I don't understand what the purpose of this was."

The author replied, "I came here because I was invited and I talked about white privilege because it's a real thing that you are actually benefiting from right now in even asking this question." The answer didn't satisfy those who had been offended, and an argument arose. The meeting broke down in disorder.

Following the event, a group of students burned copies of Capó Crucet's book on a campus grill and posted videos of the book burning on social media. (The video can be seen as part of news stories available on YouTube at "Book Burning Incident at GSU Sparks Conversation about Diversity [2019] and "GSU Holds Series of Meetings after Book Burning" [2019].) Because of the potential for violence, Georgia Southern arranged for Capó Crucet to be moved to different lodgings for the duration of her visit. False reports circulated that students had gathered outside the author's original hotel, and a subsequent event where she was supposed to appear was canceled.

In the words of Capó Crucet, "[T]he administration said they could not guarantee my safety or the safety of its students on campus because of open carry laws." ("They could not guarantee my safety," 2019.) A 2017 Georgia law lets people with a state concealed-weapons permit to carry guns on parts of public college campuses.

The university's president, Kyle Marrero, who is himself Puerto Rican, said the incidents are "another example of freedom of expression and a continuing debate of differing ideas, which are tenets of our ongoing efforts to align with our values and initiatives encompassing inclusive excellence." Representatives of the university's Department of Writing and Linguistics called "on students to remain civil in disagreement, even on difficult issues."

In the days following the incident, several activities were scheduled to address what had occurred. Faculty members from the Department of History held sessions that explored such issues as book burning, censorship, and free speech. Other professors organized a "read-in" in an effort to promote inclusiveness and foster intellectual engagement. The Student Government Association also held meetings in an attempt to heal the community.

Russell Willerton, chair of the university's Department of Writing and Linguistics, issued a statement saying, in part,

> The Department of Writing and Linguistics at Georgia Southern University is dismayed and disappointed by the uproar against author Jennine Capó Crucet, who visited Statesboro last night. . . . Last night's discussion with the author devolved into accusations of her demonstrating racism against white people. Some students burned copies of Crucet's book on campus. We assert that destructive and threatening acts do not reflect the values of Georgia Southern University. . . . Our department values stories and how they reflect parts of the human experience. We also value discussion and debate of important issues

from all sides and perspectives. We regret that Crucet's experience in Statesboro ended as it did. We call on students to remain civil in disagreement, even on difficult issues, and to make Georgia Southern University a place that we all can feel proud to represent. (Willerton, 2019)

President Marrero issued his own statement, announcing that the students involved in the book burning would not be punished. In an email sent to the campus community, he said,

From what we have been able to determine, the night's events were another example of freedom of expression and a continuing debate of differing ideas, which are tenets of our ongoing efforts to align with our values and initiatives encompassing inclusive excellence. Specific to the reported events of that evening, while it's within the students' First Amendment rights, book burning does not align with Georgia Southern's values nor does it encourage the civil discourse and debate of ideas. (cited in Baxley, 2019)

He thus drew a distinction between *freedom of expression* and *expression reflecting the values of free inquiry in higher education*. American values, in other words, may grant people the right to condemn ideas in a manner that reminds certain people of the abuses that occurred under fascist governments. Colleges and universities, however, should permit the free exchange of ideas, even those that many consider offensive.

Some members of Marrero's faculty took a different view. They "put much of the blame elsewhere. A lack of preparation, budget cuts, and insufficient foresight unwittingly spread the kindling for the spark that would come" (Ellis, 2020). The accusation was that the incident could have been and indeed was foreseen. Racially charged language had occurred at the institution before, and efforts to address these events were regarded by some as insufficient.

What the university had tried to do was to include more discussions of diversity in its first-year experience program at the same time that the very program's budget was cut in half. The result was that less than a quarter of the instructors in the program were faculty members, the rest being nonfaculty advisors, staff members, and graduate students, many of whom felt they were not adequately trained to deal with such contentious issues. One faculty member charged, "Administration set this up to fail" (Ellis, 2020).

Was the book burning and its aftermath simply a "perfect storm" of unfortunate coincidences? Or does it provide other institutions with a lesson about growing tensions between free speech and campus civility that require faculty members, administrators, and governing boards to make important decisions about the future of higher education?

THE BROADER CONTEXT

To answer these questions, it's important to realize that what happened at Georgia Southern University is far from unique. Colleges and universities of all kinds are experiencing conflicts between their desire to create a safe, civil environment for people to study and conduct research and their commitment to their rights to free speech and academic freedom. Here are just a few examples:

- Gun-rights advocate Kaitlin Bennett visited the campus of Ohio University to interview students about their knowledge (or lack thereof) about Presidents' Day. Viewing her as a provocateur, students tried various ways of disrupting her interviews, such as playing drums loudly, throwing water at her car, tossing rolls of toilet paper, and shouting. After the event, Bennett claimed that one of the protesters had thrown hot coffee in the face of her bodyguard. She also posted a video of the protests, saying "This is what happens when a Trump supporter goes to a college campus. Leftists . . . started a riot . . . and the [university police] let it happen. I think [President Trump] should strip funding from universities like this that harbor terrorists (Bennett, 2020). She also told a local newspaper, "It seems like the most liberal college in Ohio is also the most intolerant, the most disgusting, and the most horrific when it comes to diversity of opinion, and that's what we're showing here today" (Peters, 2020).
- On the campus of the University of North Carolina at Chapel Hill, a statue honoring students who died fighting for the Confederacy had long drawn protests. Those opposed to the statue, which came to be known as Silent Sam, noted that it was only erected in 1913 (long after the Civil War), that the single largest donor to the monument was the Ku Klux Klan supporter Julian Carr (who, at the statue's dedication, boasted of once having horse-whipped a black woman), and that it had become an undesirable focal point for white supremacists. In August 2018, protesters toppled the statue. University authorities removed the statue, and a debate began about what to do with it. Some wanted it returned to its original location, while others wanted the statue removed from campus entirely. In December 2018, the university's Board of Trustees recommended that $5.3 million be allocated for the construction of a new University History and Education Center that would house the statue, a recommendation that was later rejected by the university system's Board of Governors. The Sons of Confederate Veterans filed a lawsuit claiming the statue, and a second proposal was then made that the statue be donated to this group, along with a $2.5 million trust for its care and preservation. Many faculty members and students opposed this

outcome as well, arguing that the arrangement had been made in secret and amounted to a substantial donation to an organization that some on campus regarded as a hate group. In February 2020, the same judge who had approved the second agreement then blocked it on the basis that the Sons of Confederate Veterans lacked sufficient legal standing to file its lawsuit.

- The Intercultural Affairs Committee at Yale asked students to avoid wearing "culturally unaware and insensitive costumes" (Stack, 2015). The behavior demonstrated by the students was in many ways similar to that which caused a firestorm over Canadian prime minister Justin Trudeau's use of blackface make-up as part of an Aladdin costume. The committee's request at Yale prompted a heated debate over free versus insensitive speech that ended up causing at least one lecturer to resign.
- Kevin McAleenan, acting secretary of Homeland Security for the United States, was blocked from giving the keynote address at a conference on immigration at Georgetown University because of opposition to his views.
- Wesleyan University's student government cut funding for its one-hundred-and-fifty-year-old campus newsletter after it published a conservative op-ed piece.
- Comedians such as Chris Rock, Bill Maher, and Jerry Seinfeld announced that they would no longer perform on college campuses because of heckling from audience members who regarded their humor as insulting to disenfranchised groups.
- Students constantly shouted down Charles Murray, the co-author of *The Bell Curve* (Herrnstein and Murray, 1996), which argued that IQ level was a better predictor than socioeconomic status or education level in predicting income, job performance, unwed pregnancy, and crime. Many regarded the central premise of *The Bell Curve* as fundamentally racist. Murray had also argued that four-year college degrees be eliminated and be replaced by certificates of competency in specific skills.
- The governing board of the University of Wisconsin System debated whether to suspend or even expel students if they are found to have interrupted the free speech rights of their fellow students or invited speakers on multiple occasions.

Conservatives try to silence liberals. Liberals try to silence conservatives. As Jonathan Zimmerman, a professor of education and history at the University of Pennsylvania, puts it,

Roughly three-quarters of Republicans and half of Democrats reported that they censor themselves, for fear of incurring the wrath of others. At the University of Pennsylvania, where I teach, one conservative student flatly declared that his opinions were "not acceptable" on campus. "I've rarely felt comfortable expressing my own views," the student wrote. Significantly, Penn students on the left experienced similar pressures. Palestinians said that they suppressed their views of Israel, lest Jewish students denounce them as anti-Semitic. A Bernie Sanders supporter reported that a professor called Medicare for All "socialist propaganda," but the student was afraid to object. (Zimmerman, 2020)

Self-censorship has a chilling effect on the free exchange of ideas. And many academic leaders are left wondering what effect violent protests against opposing views might have on such principles as academic freedom and the right of free speech.

A DILEMMA FOR ACADEMIC LEADERS

On one side of the issue are those who argue that First Amendment rights should never be abridged in any way, particularly in higher education. Whether we agree with what someone says or not, we must never do anything that limits the scope of debate. Doing so would have a chilling effect and might prevent the discovery of important truths.

On the other side are those who argue that certain types of speech can cause serious harm if they are not limited. For example, hate speech can incite violence, disenfranchise or alienate marginalized groups, and interfere with the rights of others to obtain an education without the threat of physical harm.

There are those who regard classroom "trigger warnings," statements that certain works or topics might cause posttraumatic stress in some students, as signs that higher education has begun to coddle students rather than to challenge them. But there are also those who argue that in the highly diverse environment of the college classroom, some students have actually suffered residual effects from military service, domestic abuse, and other experiences that can lead to severe distress or even provoke violent reactions.

How do academic leaders discover the truth when opinions about this issue are so strident and contradictory? How can they develop appropriate policies that protect free speech even as they promote campus civility? These questions are so complex that they will require the rest of this book for a complete answer. But one way to begin to understand how to navigate through the dilemma they pose is to take a short quiz.

In the following table, you will find ten statements about free speech on American college campuses. Since many of these statements are about established case law in the United States, they may or may not be true of other countries. So limit your focus in this exercise to American college campuses. Circle the word TRUE if you believe the statement is more true than false. Circle the word FALSE if you believe the statement is more false than true.

There are no trick questions here. Don't overthink your responses. Your first impressions are probably the best.

Table 1.1. Quiz on Free Speech and Campus Civility

TRUE FALSE	1.	The US Department of Education's Office of Civil Rights (OCR) has no power to compel universities to police speech that is protected by the First Amendment. Public universities cannot ban speech merely because it is offensive.
TRUE FALSE	2.	Colleges and universities have a legal duty to act in such a way as to protect their students from injury.
TRUE FALSE	3.	Colleges and universities can restrict protests on their campuses with regard to their time, place, and the manner in which they occur.
TRUE FALSE	4.	It is legal for colleges and universities to punish members of their communities for engaging in certain types of speech.
TRUE FALSE	5.	Private colleges and universities may restrict freedom of speech among their members in a way that public colleges and universities cannot.
TRUE FALSE	6.	After a rash of student protests against controversial speakers on college campuses in the United States, lawmakers in several states passed legislation they say protects everyone's free speech.
TRUE FALSE	7.	There are no effective strategies to combat the potential harm of speech while still protecting free speech.
TRUE FALSE	8.	The Constitution allows public colleges and universities to cancel a student-sponsored event if the administration disagrees with the speaker's views.
TRUE FALSE	9.	If it's known that an event with a speaker may lead to physical violence, it is legal (it may even be *required*) for public colleges and universities to cancel the event.
TRUE FALSE	10.	Freedom of speech permits people to shout down a speaker when they don't agree with his or her message.

While several of these statements include matters of opinion (such as about what colleges and universities *should* do), many of them have clearly defined answers. Even the items that involve matters of opinion reflect issues about which a consensus has emerged among most professors and administrators at American universities.

Here, then, is the answer key to the quiz.

1. *The U.S. Department of Education's Office of Civil Rights (OCR) has no power to compel universities to police speech that is protected by the First Amendment. Public universities cannot ban speech merely because it is offensive.* **TRUE.** Offensive speech may be problematic but it is not

illegal. American colleges and universities cannot rely on the federal government (including the OCR) to ban speech that is otherwise protected under the First Amendment.

2. *Colleges and universities have a legal duty to act in such a way as to protect their students from injury.* **TRUE.** There are certain clear-cut instances in which institutions of higher education have the legal responsibility to provide students with a learning environment that's as safe as possible. For example, under Title IX (the congressional act that prohibits discrimination on the basis of gender in education programs that benefit from federal financial assistance), several classes of employees have a legal obligation to report alleged incidents of sexual harassment, sexual violence, and sex-based discrimination. These *mandatory reporters* include vice presidents, vice provosts, deans, department chairs, directors, and coaches. In addition, the Clery Act requires any college or university that receives federal funding to publish an annual report that includes statistics about campus crime for the preceding three calendar years and documents efforts to improve campus safety. Beyond such requirements, most college administrators and faculty members would probably argue that their schools also have a *moral* obligation to protect their students from injury.

3. *Colleges and universities can restrict protests on their campuses with regard to their time, place, and the manner in which they occur.* **TRUE.** The US Supreme Court has repeatedly upheld the right of college campuses to impose valid time, place, and manner restrictions on college protests as a way of protecting the institution's primary functions of teaching, research, and service. Nevertheless, as will be demonstrated in Chapter 3, those time, place, and manner restrictions must be reasonable and not overly broad.

4. *It is legal for colleges and universities to punish members of their communities for engaging in certain types of speech.* **TRUE.** Genuine threats (i.e., intimidating statements that aren't made in jest and that can be prosecuted under the law), harassment, destruction of property, and disruptions of classes and campus activities aren't examples of protected speech, and colleges and universities may sanction those who engage in these activities.

5. *Private colleges and universities may restrict freedom of speech among their members in a way that public colleges and universities cannot.* **TRUE.** Private institutions aren't bound by the First Amendment, which only limits government action. In particular, a religious institution may have a valid reason for requiring professors and students to adhere to its

creed, which could include restrictions on their speech and actions. Nevertheless, if a private college or university advertises itself as a bastion of free thought and expression, members of the community may argue that restrictions on their free speech are a *contractual*, not constitutional violation. Private schools should clarify their stance on freedom of thought and speech in a way that is unmistakable. Otherwise misunderstandings are likely to arise.

6. *After a rash of student protests against controversial speakers on college campuses in the United States, lawmakers in several states passed legislation they say protects everyone's free speech.* **TRUE.** As of this writing, seventeen US states have enacted this type of free speech law, eight in 2019 alone.

7. *There are no effective strategies to combat the potential harm of speech while still protecting free speech.* **FALSE.** As will become clear in later chapters of this book, one effective approach to combat the potential harm of speech is "more speech, not enforced silence." This approach protects free speech by its very nature. Moreover, the authors will also present other effective strategies that institutions have used to help preserve both freedom of speech and campus civility.

8. *The constitution allows public colleges and universities to cancel a student-sponsored event if the administration disagrees with the speaker's views.* **FALSE.** The key word in this statement is *public*. Colleges and universities that are supported at least in part by tax dollars are not permitted to cancel a student-sponsored event if the administration disagrees with the speaker's views. Private institutions, including certain faith-based colleges may exercise their right to do so, however.

9. *If it's known that an event with a speaker may lead to physical violence, it is legal (it may even be required) for public colleges and universities to cancel the event.* **FALSE.** As surprising as it may be for many people who work in higher education, canceling a speech because of fear of violence does not fall within an institution's duty to take action that will protect its students from harm. Preventing the exercise of free speech out of concern for a *potential* reaction to the speech is know legally as the *heckler's veto* and is considered a form of prior restraint.

10. *Freedom of speech permits people to shout down a speaker when they don't agree with his or her message.* **FALSE.** Freedom of speech does not give people permission to silence the speech of others by shouting, heckling, or otherwise disrupting a speech to the point that the speaker cannot continue or that the audience can no longer listen. Silencing others is not a protected form of speech under the First Amendment.

Free speech and campus civility sometimes come in conflict because well-intentioned people make decisions that have unintended consequences. They want to demonstrate their opposition to certain points of view, and so they try to silence those who disagree with them or engage in protests that violate the rights of others. Instead of using well-reasoned arguments (or mild ridicule) to point out the weaknesses in the perspectives of their opponents, they exacerbate an already tense situation through violence, the threat of violence, or what the public may *perceive* as a threat of violence.

By doing so, these protesters may actually bring more attention to the opinions they're condemning than if they simply chose to ignore them. But it can be unreasonable, particularly on a college campus where students and faculty members are often passionate about their beliefs, to expect that people will sit by idly while they feel that speakers are misrepresenting the truth.

CONCLUSION

A crisis is a period of intense challenge where an important decision must be made. A dilemma is a crisis in which none of the available options is clearly better than the others or at least comes without substantial risks. To many academic leaders, being confronted by a choice between freedom of speech and campus civility is more than just a crisis. It's a dilemma, perhaps the hardest dilemma they've ever faced in their professional lives.

In the pages that follow, a number of field-tested ideas will be examined that seek to solve this dilemma. In order to do so, however, it's important to place this entire issue into a broader context by discussing what has been called the Free Speech Movement and its impact.

KEY POINTS IN THIS CHAPTER

- Academic leaders often find themselves caught in a dilemma. They want to promote civil discourse on their campuses, but they also want to promote free speech. And free speech sometimes becomes uncivil.
- Speech does not become illegal simply because it's offensive.
- Public universities and private universities in the United States have different obligations under the First Amendment.
- Not all types of speech are protected by the First Amendment. For example, genuine threats, harassment, destruction of property, and disruptions of classes and campus activities can be sanctioned by institutional policies, state or federal law, and in some cases civil law.

- Several states in the United States have passed legislation designed to intensify federal guarantees of free speech.
- It is illegal for government entities (including public universities) to engage in prior restraint of free speech (i.e., silencing someone because of a fear that he or she will say something problematic or that violence will result).

QUESTIONS FOR REFLECTION

1. If you had been the president of Georgia Southern University when the burning of Capó Crucet's book occurred, how would you have handled the situation?
2. A number of conflicts between free speech and campus civility were mentioned in this chapter, including the forced removal of the Silent Sam statue at the University of North Carolina at Chapel Hill and the protests against Kevin McAleenan and Charles Murray. If you were an academic leader at one of the institutions where these incidents occurred, what might you have done differently from the actual actions taken by administrators?
3. Were there any answers provided to the Quiz on Free Speech and Campus Civility with which you disagreed? If so, why? Is your disagreement based on your interpretation of the *facts as they are* or the world as you believe it *should be*?

REFERENCES

Baxley, M. (2019). President Marrero addresses book burning in email. *The George-Anne.* http://www.thegeorgeanne.com/news/article_d4b5155e-ec61-11e9-bc8c-aff 75c17c05f.html.

Bennett, K. (2020). https://twitter.com/KaitMarieox/status/1229509706252738561 ?ref_src=twsrc%5Ettw%7Ctwcamp%5Etweetembed%7Ctwterm%5E1229509706 252738561&ref_url=https%3A%2F%2Fwww.insider.com%2Fkent-state-gun-girl -kaitlin-bennett-thronged-by-student-protesters-2020-2.

Book burning incident at GSU sparks conversation about diversity. (2019). https:// www.youtube.com/watch?v=7TIhF7i9ccw.

Crucet, J. C. (2016). *Make your home among strangers.* New York: Picador.

Crucet, J. C. (2019). *My time among the whites: Notes from an unfinished education.* New York: Picador.

Ellis, L. (2020). Racist incidents, budget cuts, and faculty warnings: Inside the run-up to a campus book-burning. *The Chronicle of Higher Education.* https://www .chronicle.com/article/Racist-Incidents-Budget-Cuts/247845.

GSU holds series of meetings after book burning. (2019). https://www.youtube.com/watch?v=aw2dNp71f-Q.

Herrnstein, R. J., and Murray, C. A. (1996). *The bell curve: Intelligence and class structure in American life.* New York: Simon and Schuster.

Peters, B. (2020). OU student protesters hound "gun girl" Kaitlin Bennett off campus. *The Athens News.* https://www.athensnews.com/news/campus/ou-student-protesters-run-gun-girl-kaitlin-bennett-off-campus/article_b36245f8-51d7-11ea-b03b-83117fdb5759.html.

Stack, L. (2015). Yale's Halloween advice stokes a racially charged debate. *The New York Times.* https://www.nytimes.com/2015/11/09/nyregion/yale-culturally-insensitive-halloween-costumes-free-speech.html.

"They could not guarantee my safety": Author's speech cancelled after Georgia students burn book. (2019). https://www.cbc.ca/news/entertainment/crucet-cancels-speech-book-burning-1.5319443.

Willerton, R. (2019). Department issues statement condemning book burning. https://cah.georgiasouthern.edu/writling/2019/10/10/department-issues-statement-condemning-book-burning/.

Zimmerman, J. (2020). Commentary: Free speech and college campuses: Why are students censoring themselves, and will Joe Biden help? *The Chicago Tribune.* https://www.chicagotribune.com/opinion/commentary/ct-opinion-college-political-thinking-zimmerman-20201113-ayczvbhhnvgxnh5x3olv45d2o4-story.html.

RESOURCES

Baer, U. (2019). *What snowflakes get right: Free speech and truth on campus.* New York: Oxford University Press.

Ben-Porath, S. R. (2017). *Free speech on campus.* Philadelphia: University of Pennsylvania Press.

Chemerinsky, E., and Gillman, H. (2018). *Free speech on campus.* New Haven, CT: Yale University Press.

Raphelson, S. (2017). States consider legislation to protect free speech on campus. *National Public Radio.* https://www.npr.org/2017/05/05/527092506/states-consider-legislation-to-protect-free-speech-on-campus.

Roth, M. S. (2019). *Safe enough spaces: A pragmatist's approach to inclusion, free speech, and political correctness on college campuses.* New Haven, CT: Yale University Press.

Slater, T. (2016). *Unsafe space: The crisis of free speech on campus.* London, UK: Palgrave Macmillan.

Sun, J. C., and McClellan, G. S. (2020). *Student clashes on campus: A leadership guide to free speech.* New York: Routledge, Taylor and Francis.

Chapter Two

The Free Speech Movement
and Its Impact

Our Nation is deeply committed to safeguarding academic freedom, which is of transcendent value to all of us and not merely to the teachers concerned. That freedom is therefore a special concern of the First Amendment, which does not tolerate laws that cast a pall of orthodoxy over the classroom. . . . The Nation's future depends on leaders trained through wide exposure to that robust exchange of ideas which discovers truth out of a multitude of tongues, [rather] than through any kind of authoritative selection.

—William J. Brennan, Jr., writing for the majority in the Supreme Court
Case *Keyishian v. Board of Regents*, 385 US 589 (1967)

The main task we face is preserving the university not merely as a free political community but primarily as an institution that is privileged to be an intellectual sanctuary within a society that is now in political flux. After all, the university's primary mission resides not in political activity but in the cultivation of the intellectual freedoms. . . . [A]ny conflict between the intellectual and the political way of life must be resolved in favor of the intellectual over the political.

—Professor Albert Lepawsky, speaking during the Berkeley Free Speech
Movement, 1964 (Lipset and Wolin, 1965, 22)

Campus disturbances have existed almost as long as there have been college campuses. Organized boycotts of professors who were regarded as poor teachers at the University of Bologna, commonly regarded as the oldest university in Europe, were intended to improve the quality of instruction. In 1209, a protest over a lynching in Oxford led to a strike by professors and their students that ultimately resulted in the creation of a rival university in

Cambridge. Twenty years later, a student strike at the University of Paris led to a number of institutional reforms.

The Student Representative Councils that began at British universities in the nineteenth century negotiated (often quite vocally) on behalf of their members much as graduate student labor unions do today. And many campus disturbances either changed history or sought valiantly to do so.

- In 1942, the anti-Nazi resistance movement known as the White Rose, which included Sophie Scholl and the philosophy professor Kurt Huber, developed from a secret protest group at the University of Munich.
- In 1960, the lunch counter protest held by the Greensboro Four led to the creation of the Student Nonviolent Coordinating Committee.
- In 1968, university protests broke out in the United States, France, and Poland as a resistance movement against a range of actions by the governments of those countries.
- In 1976, several thousand students near Johannesburg protested against a law mandating Afrikaans-language education, an event that is regarded by many as the beginning of the end of Apartheid.
- In 1979, a group of Iranian college students began a protest that resulted in the seizure of the American Embassy in Tehran and the taking of more than four hundred hostages.
- In 1989, prodemocracy demonstrations by students eventually led to the slaughter of hundreds of people in Tiananmen Square.
- In 2017, student protests preceded the resignation of Nicholas Dirks as chancellor of the University of California, Berkeley, prompted in part by his support for his executive vice-chancellor and provost who had been accused of mishandling a sexual harassment investigation involving the dean of the law school. During the same year, a large number of graduating seniors at Notre Dame walked out of their own graduation, protesting the selection of Vice President Mike Pence as the commencement speaker.
- In 2018, following a series of protests at the University of California, Irvine related to the #MeToo Movement, the institution removed the name of donor Francisco J. Ayala from several of its programs and buildings because of sexual harassment complaints against him.

Although many other examples could be added to this list, perhaps one of the most famous examples of campus disturbances having a lasting effect occurred in 1964 at the University of California, Berkeley. Protests over the war in Vietnam reached their climax on December 2, 1964, when, after a rally featuring the folk singer and activist Joan Baez, students occupied the administration building. This sit-in and related events continued for two months and led to the arrest of 773 people.

Many faculty members at the university supported the students and provided them with bail money. Clark Kerr, president of the University of California during these protests, refused to expel the student activists, arguing, "The University is not engaged in making ideas safe for students. It is engaged in making students safe for ideas. Thus it permits the freest expression of views before students, trusting to their good sense in passing judgment on these views. Only in this way can it best serve American democracy" (Berdahl, 2004).

Not everyone in California agreed with Kerr's approach. He was fired three weeks after Ronald Reagan took office as the governor of California in 1967.

Other universities also took different approaches. In 1968, for example, the administration building at the University of Notre Dame was the site of a sit-in by students who were protesting continued campus recruitment by Dow Chemical and the Central Intelligence Agency. There were rumors of a plan to burn down the school's ROTC building.

The president of the university, Father Theodore Hesburgh, struggled for many weeks with how best to respond to this crisis. Finally, on February 17, 1969, he sent a letter to students that was also published in the *New York Times*. In the letter, Hesburgh said,

> Youth . . . has much to offer—idealism, generosity, dedication, and service. [But t]he last thing a shaken society needs is more shaking. The last thing a noisy, turbulent, and disintegrating community needs is more noise, turbulence, and disintegration.
>
> Understanding and analysis of social ills cannot be conducted in a boiler factory. Compassion has a quiet way of service. Complicated social mechanisms, out of joint, are not adjusted with a sledge hammer.
>
> The university cannot cure all our ills today, but it can make a valiant beginning by bringing all its intellectual and moral powers to bear upon them: all the idealism and generosity of its young people, all the wisdom and intelligence of its oldsters, all the expertise and competence of those who are in their middle years. But it must do all this as a university does, within its proper style and capability, no longer an ivory tower, but not the Red Cross either. . . .
>
> I believe that I now have a clear mandate from this University community to see that: (1) our lines of communication between all segments of the community are kept as open as possible, with all legitimate means of communicating dissent assured, expanded, and protected; (2) civility and rationality are maintained; and (3) violation of another's rights or obstruction of the life of the University are outlawed as illegitimate means of dissent in this kind of open society.
>
> Now comes my duty of stating, clearly and unequivocally, what happens *if* [these standards are not met]. I'll try to make it as simple as possible to avoid

misunderstanding by anyone. Anyone or any group that substitutes force for rational persuasion, be it violent or non-violent, will be given fifteen minutes of meditation to cease and desist. They will be told that they are, by their actions, going counter to the overwhelming conviction of this community as to what is proper here.

If they do not within that time period cease and desist, they will be asked for their identity cards. Those who produce these will be suspended from this community as not understanding what this community is. Those who do not have or will not produce identity cards will be assumed not to be members of the community and will be charged with trespassing and disturbing the peace on private property and treated accordingly by the law. (Hesburgh, 1969)

Although Hesburgh's solution, which came to be known as the "Fifteen-Minute Rule," remained the university's official policy throughout the remainder of his presidency, it was only enforced once. The following November ten students were suspended for blocking a door during a protest; several of them later returned to the university and graduated, while others transferred to different universities (Fosmoe, 2019; Fromm, 1969; and Smith, 1969).

If Kerr privileged free speech over civility, Hesburgh privileged civility over free speech, and yet both believed that they were furthering principles essential to the very concept of higher education. Both their universities also drew national attention as the site of later protests that some regarded as attempts to restrict free speech.

FREE SPEECH AND ACADEMIC FREEDOM

One of the reasons why the issue of free speech at colleges and universities is so much more complex than it is at other institutions is that the topics of free speech and academic freedom are so intertwined. Any attempt to restrict what one says in higher education, even in the cause of promoting greater civility or community, is regarded by some as a restriction of scholars to "speak the truth" as they see it.

There are few topics in higher education more widely cherished, more widely discussed, and more widely misunderstood than academic freedom. Part of this misunderstanding arises because the expression *academic freedom* is used in two not entirely identical ways. *Institutional* academic freedom is the right that schools have to determine their own mission without governmental interference and to control such matters as what they will teach, who will teach it, and which students will be accepted for admission.

Individual academic freedom refers to the right of members of an academic community to pursue areas of research without unwarranted interference and to engage in pedagogy guided by proper professional standards, not governmental decree.

The most important summary of what academic freedom is—and also what its limits are—is the 1940 *Statement of Principles on Academic Freedom and Tenure* by the American Association of University Professors (AAUP), clarified in 1970 by the addition of several "interpretive comments." The goal of this statement was to advocate a reasonable balance between rights and responsibilities in the area of individual academic freedom. For example,

- *Teaching*: College professors should be entitled to discuss matters relevant to their discipline however they wish in accordance with their best professional judgment. They should, however, refrain from introducing "controversial" matter into their courses that is not relevant to the subject being taught.
- *Research*: College professors should be entitled to conduct research according to the professional standards of their disciplines and to publish those results. They should, however, refrain from violating institutional guidelines governing research that is paid for by external entities.
- *Service*: College professors should be entitled to serve their communities by providing professional opinions about topics of public concern. They should, however, refrain from giving the impression that they are speaking on behalf of the institution when they are only expressing their own opinions (American Association of University Professors [AAUP], n.d.).

In a similar way, the AAUP noted that institutions also had responsibilities to its constituents with regard to academic freedom and freedom of speech. For example, if a religious institution sought to place limits on the subjects that professors could teach, the pedagogical methods they could use, the areas of research they could pursue, or the views they could express publicly, those restrictions "should be clearly stated in writing at the time of the appointment" (AAUP, n.d.).

In 1970, because of changes in both law and public opinion, the AAUP added a number of comments and clarifications to its 1940 statement. For example, it clarified that the statement's encouragement of professors to refrain from "controversial" material irrelevant to the course was not a rejection of controversial material that was indeed related to the subject matter being taught. "Controversy," the association noted, "is at the heart of the free academic inquiry which the entire statement is designed to foster" (AAUP, n.d.).

The AAUP also declared that "[m]ost church-related institutions no longer need or desire the departure from the principle of academic freedom implied in the 1940 'Statement,' and we do not now endorse such a departure" (AAUP, n.d.).

That change may have seemed appropriate in 1970, the start of a decades-long period when many church-related schools were loosening their affiliations with the denominations that had created them, but it seems less appropriate now. Beginning in the Reagan era and continuing into the twenty-first century, several colleges and universities have *intensified* their commitment to faith-based values, essentially "doubling down" on the principle that, in certain matters, faith must outweigh academic freedom.

Milligan College in northeast Tennessee states that, on its campus "each course is taught with an awareness of how it fits into a biblical worldview. . . . Such teaching is assured by the selection of a faculty who are strong and active in their Christian faith" (A Christ Centered College, 2020). Gordon College, just north of Boston, "expects that all members of the College community [including the faculty and staff] will: Call themselves Christian by virtue of the grace of God and their personal commitment to Jesus Christ. [And] Recognize the Bible to be the Word of God and hence fully authoritative in matters of faith and conduct" (Life and Conduct, 2017).

Shorter University in Rome, Georgia, requires all employees to sign a Personal Lifestyle Statement before they are hired. This statement affirms that the employee recognizes the university will only employ:

> persons who are committed Bible believing Christians, who are dedicated to integrating biblical faith in their classes and who are in agreement with the University Statement of Faith. Moreover, employees are expected to be active members of a local church. . . . I have read and agree with the Personal Lifestyle Statement and will adhere to it in its entirety while employed at Shorter University. I understand that failure to adhere to this statement may result in disciplinary action against me, up to and including immediate termination. (Personal Lifestyle Statement, n.d.)

In its nondiscrimination policy, Liberty University in Lynchburg, Virginia, states that "Liberty University maintains its Christian mission and reserves its right to discriminate on the basis of religion to the extent that applicable law respects its right to act in furtherance of its religious objectives" (Liberty University Non-Discrimination Policy, 2020).

It is interesting to note that Liberty University, under its original name Lynchburg Baptist College, was founded in 1971, immediately *after* the AAUP's declaration that church-related schools "no longer need or desire [a] departure from the principle of academic freedom." In the years that followed, Liberty continued to resist the trend of many other schools to break from their local religious conventions or denominations in order to retain more autonomy and develop a more multicultural curriculum.

Rather than threatening academic freedom, however, the existence of these church-related schools actually *strengthens* it. It means that, if faculty members want to teach and conduct research at an institution from a specific religious perspective—and if students want to study issues solely from that perspective—they are free to apply to these schools. If they don't wish to do so, they're free to work or study elsewhere.

Indeed, all of the religious schools mentioned here are only a short drive away from public colleges or universities or private nonreligious universities that, by law, must allow all members of the faculty, staff, and student body to follow any religion they wish or no religion at all. In certain cases, strictly religious and strictly secular institutions are even walking distance from one another.

The existence of all these different schools represents one of the strengths of American higher education (and higher education in many other countries as well): its diversity. People who wish to study within a certain tradition have that option. People who wish to be exposed to many different traditions also have that option. People who wish to see traditions challenged or perhaps even shaken to their foundations have that option as well. Academic freedom, freedom of speech, and freedom of thought are maintained through diversity. One of the lasting legacies of the Free Speech Movement has been a commitment in higher education to that very spirit of diversity.

INSTITUTIONS AND VALUES

The emphasis on Christian values demonstrated by schools like Milligan College, Shorter University, and Liberty University does raise another issue, however. Is the purpose of higher education simply to provide students with facts, figures, and critical thinking skills, or may institutions also see their purpose as the transmission of values? As constitutional law scholar Alan Brownstein notes,

> Secular institutions are condemned for entrenching orthodoxy in who they hire, what professors teach and write about, and even who may be invited to speak on campus. If you hold and espouse the "wrong" beliefs about racial and gender equality, access to abortion, LGBTQ rights and numerous other issues, critics argue, you are not welcome on campus. Religious colleges and universities also entrench orthodoxy of belief and exclude those whose values conflict with the tenets of their faith. These schools, however, are more likely to be praised

for the values-centered education they provide rather than challenged for their exclusionary policies. (Brownstein, 2020)

Although Brownstein specifically notes that he is speaking here only of secular *private* colleges, one might well make the same points about public universities as well. Is their purpose the transmission of all ideas or only ideas that have been tested through critical analysis and an examination of available evidence? Moreover, if an institution claims that it is not merely teaching facts and figures but also building the *character* of its students, isn't it appropriate for the school to say that certain values reflect the principles it wishes to convey while others don't?

This issue is one that will need to be explored further in Chapter 6, but it's appropriate to emphasize at this point that academic leaders face something of a dilemma. If they claim that colleges exist to expose students to a full and unexpurgated range of ideas, then shouldn't speakers who wish to speak about the immanence of a zombie apocalypse or the role of aliens in building the Egyptian pyramids also be invited to campus? Shouldn't speakers who deny the scientific method and basic mathematical principles be given a voice in classrooms?

On the other hand, if colleges exist only to expose students to ideas that have been refined and tested, then who sets the standards for the "test" that is used? Professors in the natural sciences will claim that they deal in theories, not mere hypotheses, and use the rigor of the scientific method to weed out ideas that have little or no merit. But don't scholars in the arts, humanities, and social sciences also have ways of testing hypotheses before they become theories? And is it really appropriate to privilege the methodology of the natural sciences over the methodologies of other disciplines?

FREE SPEECH AND THE INTERNET

Electronic communication has added an entirely new dimension to the issue of free speech and civility. Public shaming and bullying in social media aren't phenomena that are limited to schoolchildren. College professors have used the internet to bully and shame their colleagues, and administrators have used the internet to pressure and manipulate the faculty.

The first thing that people in higher education need to understand is that the medium does not change the essential contours of free speech and its restrictions. Threats and defamation are still threats and defamation regardless of whether they're spoken, written, or posted online. Social media sites are sometimes represented as being "like the Wild West" where anything can go, and the rules don't apply, but that simply isn't the case.

One factor that does make the internet different from other media for communication is the fact that the most popular sites tend to be operated by private companies. That means that, like religious colleges and universities, they have greater freedom to set their own rules irrespective of the First Amendment. Facebook, Twitter, Instagram, YouTube, and other social media sites are not governmental agencies, and so they can allow or disallow whatever they wish to be distributed through their servers.

Consider two venues for speech. The first is a "Hyde Park Corner" type of opportunity in a city-owned public park where anyone who wishes may voice an opinion there. The second is Professor Skeptic's physical chemistry class. A self-proclaimed alchemist who wishes to present a new idea for turning lead into gold is perfectly free to present those ideas at the designated location in the public park. But that doesn't mean that the alchemist gets to offer a rebuttal in Professor Skeptic's class. The park is a venue for unfiltered ideas; the classroom is a venue for filtered ideas. In the case of the hypothetical example described here, the filter used consists of professional standards in physical chemistry and accreditation standards for the institution.

A social media site is more like Professor Skeptic's class than it is like Hyde Park Corner. The operator of the site is allowed to filter the speech disseminated there. But unlike the imaginary physical chemistry class, the filters that can be used aren't limited to professional or accreditation standards. Privately owned social media companies can filter speech by any standards they wish.

If a social media site decided to block dissemination of all postings that advocate a conservative worldview, they are perfectly free to do so. The *site* has freedom of speech; not the person using that site. But it could just as easily block dissemination of all postings that advocate a liberal worldview. The point is that the website is a privately owned company; it's not the government and, as noted previously, the First Amendment only applies to governmental speech.

These principles were tested in 2020 when President Trump was angered that Twitter attached fact-checking notices to several of his tweets. On May 29, 2020, the president tweeted,

> Twitter is doing nothing about all of the lies & propaganda being put out by China or the Radical Left Democrat Party. They have targeted Republicans, Conservatives & the President of the United States. Section 230 should be revoked by Congress. Until then, it will be regulated! (Trump, 2020)

In the executive order Trump signed as a result of these events, he noted,

> The growth of online platforms in recent years raises important questions about applying the ideals of the First Amendment to modern communications

technology. Today, many Americans follow the news, stay in touch with friends and family, and share their views on current events through social media and other online platforms. As a result, these platforms function in many ways as a 21st century equivalent of the public square. . . . Online platforms are engaging in selective censorship that is harming our national discourse. Tens of thousands of Americans have reported, among other troubling behaviors, online platforms "flagging" content as inappropriate, even though it does not violate any stated terms of service; making unannounced and unexplained changes to company policies that have the effect of disfavoring certain viewpoints; and deleting content and entire accounts with no warning, no rationale, and no recourse (Executive Order, 2020).

The problem with these statements is that they neglect the fact that the First Amendment doesn't apply to private companies like Twitter any more than it applies to the alchemist who claims a "right" to lecture in Professor Skeptic's class. It may be someone's personal *opinion* that social media sites are the "21st century equivalent of the public square," but as a statement of fact it is wrong. In the eyes of the law, a private company and a public square are wholly different types of entity. Saying that anyone has the right to post any opinion they want on social media is far more like saying anyone has the right to spray paint any slogan they want on the walls of your bedroom than it is like protection against censorship (see Franks, 2020; and Tribe and Geltzer, 2020).

In January 2021, Twitter and Facebook indefinitely suspended Donald Trump's accounts because they had repeatedly disseminated false statements.

A HYPOTHETICAL CASE STUDY

It is difficult, perhaps even impossible, for academic leaders to know what choices they'll make when confronted by an actual conflict between free speech and academic freedom on the one side and civility and public order on the other. People who feel that academic freedom is the most important of their core values and that civility is a fine thing but not essential may end up making quite different choices when faced with a campus protest on the verge of becoming a riot. Those who, like Father Hesburgh, regard the reasoned exchange of ideas as the very foundation of the university may be surprised to find themselves trying to shout down their opponents when legislatures and governing boards seek to dictate what must and what cannot be said in a classroom.

Having to make choices when core values come into conflict with one another is an important device for determining whether your academic leadership is truly authentic or merely based on principles to which you're giving only lip service. (See, for example, Buller 2018.) But the middle of a crisis may not be the best time either for you or for your institution to discover what your unshakable commitments actually are.

For this reason, the consideration of hypothetical case studies can be an effective way of envisioning how you might react without having to suffer (or, for that matter, having the opportunity to benefit from) those reactions. As a device for clarifying your own approaches to the tensions between free speech and campus civility, several of these case studies will be used in this book. As in real life, some hypothetical case studies have multiple possible solutions, no possible solutions, or a range of solutions, some of which are better than others. Some hypothetical case studies are more like "test cases" in which one particular approach is far more likely to lead to the most desirable outcome.

The first case study in this book falls into the last category. Read it over and answer the questions that follow it.

Dr. Upton O. Goode, chair of the Department of Organic Astral Therapy at Dicey Incline State University (DISU), has invited Ms. Stuckin D'Past, the founder of a group that's widely perceived as advocating white nationalism, to deliver a campus address on current challenges facing society. Dr. Goode has required all students majoring in organic astral therapy to attend, opened his own courses to Ms. D'Past for further discussion, and invited all other students to attend the public lecture.

The title that Ms. D'Past has chosen for her speech, "The Crime of Diversity," has attracted concern from students, faculty, and administrators alike. A large majority of those on campus believe that the speech will support the agenda for white nationalism and encourage violence. The League of Students for Diversity (LSD) has planned a massive protest at the event and reached out to DISU students, employees, and members of the community to join them. LSD has stated in emails that it intends to disrupt the event—by any and all means possible—to stop Ms. D'Past from speaking.

Mr. Barry D. Hatchett, the president of DISU, is afraid that if the speech is allowed to proceed, violence will erupt that his campus's security service will be unable to contain. The rhetoric around Ms. D'Past's appearance has become so strident that the local mayor and town council believe public safety may be at risk.

Several outside groups, both supportive of and opposed to Ms. D'Past's group, have threatened to appear at the public event and advocate for their causes. President Hatchett is on the verge of canceling the presentation entirely when he receives an email from Dr. Goode indicating that any attempt by the administration to block Ms. D'Past from speaking would be regarded as violating the First Amendment and its guarantees of free speech as well as Dr. Goode's own academic freedom.

An official statement by Ms. D'Past said that she hoped all "right thinking" members of the community would come to the event and demonstrate their support of her right to speak and opposition to the "fascist tactics" of groups like LSD. Hearing the responses to this statement from listeners to call-in radio, President Hatchett becomes even more concerned about what might happen at the public event.

The president knows he must act quickly since the day of Ms. D'Past's arrival is rapidly approaching. He calls his cabinet into a joint session with his governing board and tries to work out a plan for how to proceed. The group makes the following accommodations. DISU will:

- Budget an additional $250,000 (taken from funds originally set aside for staff bonuses) for police to attend and monitor the public event and do what they can to prevent violence.
- Offer Ms. D'Past a "safe space" to deliver her presentation.
- Publicize the fact that the First Amendment does not provide anyone with the right to disrupt campus activities.
- Establish bias response teams (BRTs) to monitor this event and similar activities in the future that have the potential for resulting in violence.
- Take a public stance that freedom of speech allows people to state their opinions without interference, retaliation, or punishment from the government.

QUESTIONS

1. What is your opinion of this proposed solution? Is this solution the one that you would adopt if you were in President Hatchett's position?
2. If the proposed solution is not what you would do, what course of action would you take instead?
3. Are there parts of President Hatchett's plan that are better than others?
4. What would you do if you were each of the following?
   a. Dr. Goode, the faculty member who originally invited the external speaker
   b. The president of DISU's faculty senate
   c. The president of the LSD
   d. The chair of the governing board
   e. The director of campus safety at DISU
   f. The mayor of the city where DISU is located
   g. The chief of police of the city where DISU is located

To make the best use of this case study, decide what your own answers would be before proceeding to the following discussion.

Certainly there are different approaches you might take with regard to the hypothetical situation at DISU. Academic leaders all approach challenges differently, based on their own experience and the traditions at their universities. But this case study is one where certain attempted solutions may cause the situation to become even worse.

First, it's important to identify where the central issue in this case study lies. People merely *believe* that Ms. D'Past's speech will support the agenda for white nationalism and encourage violence, but Ms. D'Past herself hasn't said so. On the other hand, the LSD has *explicitly* threatened in emails that it intends to disrupt the event by any and all means possible. Canceling the public event would thus involve prior restraint of free speech, which is illegal, but LSD's documented incitement of others to violence or lawless action is not protected free speech and may suitably be investigated by the police.

Second, while President Hatchett is justifiably concerned about the safety of his faculty and students, many of the solutions proposed by his cabinet and governing board take only a short-term approach. With the exception of creating BRTs (themselves questionable because they appear to be designed for prior restraint of free speech), none of the proposed actions involve substantive, long-term approaches.

Instead, DISU should also consider developing publications or web pages that explain what free speech is, what "time, place, and manner" restrictions are, and how the institution will both protect free speech and address expressions that are deemed threats or incitements to violence. In other words, DISU should make this challenge a teachable moment. Best practices in how to do so will be explored in Chapter 3.

Third, President Hatchett should consider launching a program that educates students—as well as faculty members and administrators—on how differences of opinion can be expressed constructively and how to discuss sensitive or contentious issues. Crises like the one described in the case study are moments when the need for effective academic leadership is at its greatest. President Hatchett may have tried valiantly to demonstrate that leadership but he would be better advised to begin a campus-wide dialog on how free speech, academic freedom, and public safety can all be pursued together. Best practices in how to accomplish this goal will be explored in Chapter 4.

CONCLUSION

Free speech on college and university campuses will continue to present significant challenges to academic leaders. As with so many of today's issues, there is no "one size fits all" strategy that can bring about a perfect accommodation between campus civility and free speech. But some ideas are better than others. There are best practices that already exist at many institutions of higher education, and academic leaders can learn from those practices to develop an approach that best serves the mission, tradition, and needs of their own schools.

Addressing the challenges academic leaders face will require a great deal of effort, compromise, and mutual understanding on the part of students, faculty members, and administrators alike if the goal is to promote truly free scholarly inquiry while simultaneously creating a culture of respect for those who oppose other people's ideas. It will also require dialogue. In the chapters that follow, practical advice on how to begin that dialogue will be examined in greater detail.

KEY POINTS IN THIS CHAPTER

- The phenomenon of campus incivility arising from protests is not a recent development. It has existed for as long as there have been universities.
- Many current perspectives about what campus incivility means were, however, shaped by the events that led to the Free Speech Movement, which arose at the University of California, Berkeley, in the 1960s.
- The approaches taken in the 1960s by Clark Kerr at the University of California System and Father Theodore Hesburgh at the University of Notre Dame represent in many ways two contrasting poles in the conflict between free speech and campus civility.
- There are actually two types of academic freedom: *institutional* academic freedom, which refers to the rights that schools have to determine their own mission without governmental interference, and *individual* academic freedom, which refers to the right of professors to pursue areas of research without unwarranted interference and to engage in pedagogy guided solely by proper professional standards.
- The AAUP 1940 *Statement of Principles on Academic Freedom and Tenure*, clarified in 1970, serves as the leading document many institutions use today for what academic freedom means and where the rights of academic freedom end.

- In the United States, private, church-affiliated schools are not restricted by the First Amendment's guarantees of freedom of speech in the same way that public colleges and universities are.
- At schools where freedom of speech is protected, prior restraint of speech may not be imposed, but the school is entitled to specify the time, place, and manner in which protests or large gatherings may occur.

QUESTIONS FOR REFLECTION

1. As you read the different responses to campus protests by Clark Kerr and Theodore Hesburgh, did you find yourself agreeing more with one approach than the other? If so, why?
2. Mary Spellman, the dean of students at Claremont McKenna College, resigned in 2015 after a protest over an email in which she promised a Latinx student that she'd work to serve those who "don't fit our CMC mold." At the same institution, the junior class president also resigned after protests arose over a Halloween photo in which she posed with two blonde women in sombreros and mustaches, holding maracas. Both Spellman and the junior class president believed that what they did was well intentioned, although it was viewed as disrespectful by others. Do you regard the resignations as appropriate, an over-reaction to so-called "political correctness," a combination of the two, or something else entirely?
3. Certain authors, such as Kirsten Powers in *The Silencing* (2015), argue that the attempts to exclude voices from college campuses today is largely one sided, that it's predominantly liberals who seek to silence conservative and libertarian voices. Has that been your experience? If there have been campus disturbances over expressions of views at any institution where you yourself had worked, was the object of the protest a liberal person or group or a conservative person or group?
4. The term *confirmation bias* refers to a tendency to disregard evidence that may contradict or undermine an opinion we already hold. A similar concept, *diagnosis bias*, refers to a tendency, after we label a person or condition, to ignore evidence to the contrary. To what extent do you believe that confirmation bias and diagnosis bias may affect the way in which people interpret whether a campus conflict is appropriate or undesirable?

REFERENCES

A Christ Centered College: Milligan College. (2020). https://www.milligan.edu/academics/a-christ-centered-college/.

American Association of University Professors (AAUP). (n.d.) 1940 statement of principles on academic freedom and tenure. https://www.aaup.org/report/1940-statement-principles-academic-freedom-and-tenure.

Berdahl, R. M. (2004). Clark Kerr memorial. https://chancellor.berkeley.edu/chancellors/berdahl/speeches/clark-kerr-memorial.

Brownstein, A. (2020). Making sense of 'orthodoxy' at secular and religious colleges. *The Hill.* https://thehill.com/opinion/education/525463-making-sense-of-orthodoxy-at-secular-and-religious-colleges.

Buller, J. L. (2018). *Authentic academic leadership: A values-based approach to college administration.* Lanham, MD: Rowman and Littlefield.

Executive Orders: Executive Order on Preventing Online Censorship. (2020). https://www.whitehouse.gov/presidential-actions/executive-order-preventing-online-censorship/.

Fosmoe, M. (2019). Fifteen minutes, 50 years later. *Notre Dame Magazine.* https://magazine.nd.edu/stories/fifteen-minutes-50-years-later/.

Franks, M. A. (2020). The utter incoherence of Trump's battle with Twitter. *The Atlantic.* https://www.theatlantic.com/ideas/archive/2020/05/the-utter-incoherence-of-trumps-battle-with-twitter/612367/.

Fromm, D. (1969, November 19). Fifteen minute rule enacted for the first time. *The Observer, 4*(46), 1, 8. http://archives.nd.edu/Observer/v04/1969-11-19_v04_046.pdf.

Hesburgh, T. M. (1969). Hesburgh letter, *New York Times.* https://hesburgh.nd.edu/fr-teds-life/the-notre-dame-president/the-60s-and-student-activism/hesburgh-letter-the-new-york-times/.

Lipset, S. M., and Wolin, S. S. (eds.) (1965). *The Berkeley student revolt: Facts and interpretations.* New York: Doubleday Anchor.

Liberty University Non-Discrimination Policy. (2020). https://www.liberty.edu/online-at-liberty/non-discrimination-policy/.

Life and Conduct: Gordon College. (2017). https://www.gordon.edu/images/html_email/admissions/application/life_conduct.htm

Personal Lifestyle Statement: Shorter University. (n.d.) https://www.shorter.edu/wp-content/uploads/personal_lifestyle_statement.pdf.

Powers, K. (2015). *The silencing: How the left is killing free speech.* Washington, DC: Regnery.

Smith, R. (1969, November 24). Dow-CIA controversy continues. *The Observer, 4*(49), 1.

Tribe, L. H., and Geltzer, J. A. (2020, May 28). Trump is doubly wrong about Twitter. *Washington Post.* https://www.washingtonpost.com/opinions/2020/05/28/trump-is-doubly-wrong-about-twitter/.

Trump, D. (2020). Tweet from May 29, 2020. https://twitter.com/realDonaldTrump/status/1266326065833824257.

RESOURCES

Cohen, R., and Zelnik, R. E. (2003). *The free speech movement: Reflections on Berkeley in the 1960s.* Berkeley: University of California Press.

Douglas, T.-R. M. O. (2020). *Campus uprisings: How student activists and collegiate leaders resist racism and create hope.* New York: Teachers College Press.

Miscamble, W. D. (2019). *American priest: The ambitious life and conflicted legacy of Notre Dame's Father Ted Hesburgh.* New York: Image.

Chapter Three

The Teachable Moment

Defining Free Speech and Its Limits

In Chapter 1, a *dilemma* was defined as a crisis in which none of the available options is clearly better than the others, or at least none of those options comes without substantial risks. Does the tension between free speech and campus civility form a genuine dilemma for academic leaders, or are there actually some approaches to this issue that are more effective than others?

Best practices already in place at certain institutions, reinforced by ongoing research into conflict resolution and successful negotiation strategies, suggest that there are three techniques that academic leaders should adopt more broadly.

1. Recognize that the tension between free speech and campus civility stems from the very mission of higher education and transform the debate from a conflict between irreconcilable ideas into a teachable moment.
2. Move beyond narrowly focused strategic planning to more broadly based scenario planning so that constructive approaches are ready if and when destructive tension between free speech and campus civility reemerges.
3. Embed exploration of free speech and civil discourse throughout the curriculum and co-curriculum by developing activities that include faculty, staff, students, and administration.

In the next three chapters, each of these ideas will be explored individually.

THE NEED FOR TEACHABLE MOMENTS

One of the reasons why free speech and campus civility so often appear to be in conflict is that different groups talk past one another instead of communicating with one another. They use terms like *academic freedom*, *freedom of speech*, *civility*, and *collegiality* in different ways, sometimes producing destructive conflict because they are either saying the same thing in different words or using the same words but meaning very different things.

Part of the solution to this problem can be, therefore, to regard campus disputes not as a type of civil disorder that should be "controlled," but as an opportunity to teach people what different terms actually mean and how they are approached in such fields as psychology, sociology, and the law. The advantage of this approach is that it is rooted in the very purpose of higher education: to provide advanced development of the human mind to meet the challenges of life.

Part of this development, many might argue, must include the ability to overcome the polarization that divides people in ways that renders them unable to act collectively for the common good. One of the trends monitored by the Pew Research Center is the degree to which the gap between people with liberal or conservative points of view changes over time.

Pew has tracked, for instance, a growing divide among self-proclaimed Republicans and Democrats on such issues as whether higher education has a generally positive effect on society (Parker, 2019); whether the views of scientists are relevant in policy debates (Kennedy and Funk, 2019); and whether leaders in government, the military, religious life, and business ought to be trusted (Rainie, Keeter, and Perrin, 2019). In each case, the research center found that the gap between liberals and conservatives is wide and growing.

One possible method colleges and universities can use to help bridge these gaps is to provide students with a shared vocabulary regardless of their political views and to teach them how to continue the development of their analytical and research skills after they graduate. These goals don't have to be accomplished solely in the classroom. Public lectures, club activities, and even campus posters or websites can also be used to foster a larger community of understanding.

UNDERSTANDING THE IMPORTANCE
OF ACADEMIC FREEDOM

As was indicated in Chapter 2, the term *academic freedom* is applied to two not entirely synonymous concepts: the right of an institution to determine its own curriculum and the right of individual faculty members to engage in research and teaching without undue government interference.

The American Association of University Professors (AAUP) declares its mission to be:

to advance academic freedom and shared governance; to define fundamental professional values and standards for higher education; to promote the economic security of faculty, academic professionals, graduate students, post-doctoral fellows, and all those engaged in teaching and research in higher education; to help the higher education community organize to make our goals a reality; and to ensure higher education's contribution to the common good (About the AAUP, n.d.).

In pursuit of this goal of serving as an advocate for academic professionals rather than institutions, it quite rightly tends to emphasize the importance of individual academic freedom rather than the freedom of colleges and universities to establish their own missions or of administrators to enforce institutional policies.

In fact, the AAUP at times almost equates institutional and individual academic freedom. For example, the association states

Academic freedom is the indispensable requisite for unfettered teaching and research in institutions of higher education. As the academic community's core policy document states, "institutions of higher education are conducted for the common good and not to further the interest of either the individual teacher or the institution as a whole. The common good depends upon the free search for truth and its free exposition." (Protecting Academic Freedom, n.d., quoting AAUP, n.d.)

The problem is that there are times when these two types of academic freedom may come in conflict with one another, particularly at public colleges and universities.

Institutional academic freedom is based on the rights of colleges and universities to have autonomy in areas for which they, and not the government, are the experts. It entitles them to set their own standards for admission, retention, and graduation, to decide what to teach and who shall teach it, and to make critical decisions about academic policy matters without the fear that those decisions will be overturned by the court.

Individual academic freedom is based on the expectation of scholars that these rights will extend to them *in their professional capacity* as academics. Physicists are entitled to explore with students how the universe came into being and to expect that they accept widely recognized scientific principles until those principles are disproved through the scientific method (if they ever are). Political scientists are not entitled to impose their views about intelligent design upon their students because that topic falls outside their area of professional expertise.

On the other hand, political scientists may well be expected to explore with their students highly controversial matters of public debate because doing so *does* fall within the area of their expertise. Physicists are *not* entitled to do so. Colleges and universities have mechanisms in place for making sure that these expectations are followed. The syllabus for a course must be approved in advance, usually at several levels of the institution, to make sure that course content aligns with the expertise of those who will teach it. If a professor deviates from that syllabus, he or she may be subject to sanctions ranging from a warning by a supervisor to, in certain extreme cases, termination if violations of this policy are frequent or particularly egregious.

These two types of freedom come into conflict with one another when a faculty member's professional judgment differs in a significant way from the institution's right to govern itself in academic matters. For example, certain branches of sociology and anthropology seek not only to understand human behavior but also to influence it. If a faculty member believes that his or her professional judgment requires recommending that students engage in public protest of a certain law or policy, while the institution believes that the maintenance or order on its property requires that public protests be limited in their time, place, or manner, the potential for a conflict of freedom arises.

Over time, courts in the United States have developed protocols for dealing with these conflicts. Perhaps the most famous of these protocols is commonly called the Pickering Balancing Test, the Pickering Connick Test, or the Garcetti-Pickering Balancing Test. The reason for these multiple titles is that, as with many other legal matters, the test is refined and modified by case law as it occurs.

The heart of the Pickering Balancing Test (as it will be known in this book) is the attempt to balance "the employee's free speech rights against the public employer's interest in operational efficiency in employment retaliation cases" (Oluwole, 2008, 133). Note the key word *public* in the description of the employer for the Pickering Balancing Test. This protocol only applies to public universities. Private institutions have far broader rights in limiting the free speech of employees, and the recourse a faculty member would have to a perceived violation of his or her rights would be a civil case based on the violation of a contract (provided that academic freedom was included in the terms of that contract), not a criminal case based on Pickering.

The Pickering Balancing Test works like this. Phase one of the test involves two questions: Did the employee speak about a matter of public concern? And did the employee speak as a private citizen rather than solely as an employee? If the answer to either question is *no*, the "balance" tilts in the direction of the employer. Since the issue had little relevance as a public concern, the employee was speaking in his or her role as an employee (and thus as a representative of the employer), or both, the employer's interest in operational efficiency is given preference.

But if the answer to both phase one questions is *yes*, the Pickering Balancing Test proceeds to phase two: Did the employer have adequate justification for treating the employee differently from any other member of the public based on the government's needs as an employer? To put this question another way, did the employer have a legitimate and demonstrable interest that was harmed by the employee's speech? If no harm was done, then the employee's right to free speech remains paramount. If there was actual harm, the rights of the employer take precedence.

With regard to individual academic freedom, therefore, the following issues have to be considered.

- Does the faculty member's speech fall within his or her professional area of specialty?
- Does the faculty member's speech fall within the context of the course as set forth in an approved course syllabus?
- If neither is the case, was the faculty member speaking as a private citizen rather than as an employee of the college or university?
- Did the faculty member's speech cause legitimate and demonstrable harm to the college or university, such as by instigating a riot that damaged property, preventing students from fulfilling the requirements of their program, or producing some other result that restricted the institution's ability to fulfill its mission?

Case law regarding *institutional* academic freedom has resulted in relatively clear guidelines. But as these questions suggest, *individual* academic freedom is more a matter of academic tradition than constitutional protection. When the First Amendment to the US Constitution becomes relevant in these issues is where individual academic freedom enters the realm of freedom of speech generally. For that reason, stakeholders of a college or university also need to understand the role that free speech plays in this issue.

UNDERSTANDING THE IMPORTANCE
OF FREEDOM OF SPEECH

If you ask most people about the rights of free speech in the United States, they'll tell you that they know two things: Free speech is protected under the First Amendment to the US Constitution and that right is limited because "you can't shout 'Fire!' in a crowded theater." Actually, the matter is a little more complicated than that.

The First Amendment does protect freedom of speech. It also offers similar protections for religious belief and assembly, provides freedom of the press (and, by extension, publication or dissemination of views in general), and gives people the right "to petition the Government for a redress of grievances." And there are indeed certain limitations to those rights. A person can't disseminate child pornography while claiming exemption under "freedom of the press," and people can't start their own religion that entitles them to murder, rape, and pillage at will while expecting the First Amendment to protect them.

But there's also a great deal of misunderstanding about the relationship of freedom of speech to the First Amendment. Some of this confusion is trivial, but other misinterpretation is quite significant. An example of a fairly trivial misunderstanding is the widespread belief that the wording about "not shouting 'Fire' in a crowded theater" can be attributed to Oliver Wendell Holmes. Holmes actually did write the unanimous opinion in the case of *Schenck v. United States*, 249 US 47 (1919), but his phrasing wasn't precisely as people remember it. The actual opinion written by Holmes states, "The most stringent protection of free speech would not protect a man in falsely shouting fire in a theatre and causing a panic."

Although minor, the differences in this phrasing do have legal implications. What Holmes was excluding from protection under the First Amendment is *falsely* making a statement and thus *causing a panic*. If the building is truly on fire, there's nothing wrong with drawing the attention of others to the situation. In fact, that would be the public-minded thing to do. And the word *crowded* doesn't appear in the statement. Even a false claim that doesn't result in "causing a panic"—or isn't, in the other famous phrase that appears later in the ruling, "a clear and present danger"—isn't specifically excluded from constitutional protection.

These minor distinctions may interest constitutional scholars, but they're unlikely to affect the decisions we make at a college or university. The more significant misunderstandings about *Schenck v. United States* should, however, concern academic leaders. What people often forget is the context of the case and thus the *type* of speech that Oliver Wendell Holmes and the other members of the Supreme Court declared not to be protected speech.

Charles T. Schenck was an officer in the Socialist Party of America, which had printed and distributed about fifteen thousand leaflets opposing the establishment of a military draft in the country. The "clear and present danger" Schenck was convicted of creating was a violation of the 1917 Espionage Act that forbade anyone from causing or attempting to cause "insubordination, disloyalty, mutiny, or *refusal of duty*, in the military or naval forces of the United States, or [from] willfully obstruct[ing] the recruiting or enlistment service of the United States" (National Archives Catalog, 1917; emphasis added). The Supreme Court ruled unanimously that Schenck's arrest and conviction were legal.

In short, what many of those who cite the trope about shouting "Fire!" in a theater don't realize is (1) Holmes used that expression in a case that *limited* the right of free speech and (2) that those limits included restrictions on the right to protest against government actions, such as the drafting of civilians. Moreover, the Schenck ruling was partially overturned in 1969.

In the case of *Brandenburg v. Ohio*, the plaintiff, Clarence Brandenburg, challenged his conviction under a state law forbidding association "with any society, group, or assemblage of persons formed to teach or advocate" the performance of criminal acts with the intent of producing social or political change (*Brandenburg v. Ohio*, 2020). Brandenburg was a leader in the Ku Klux Klan, and he gave a speech in which he noted that, if the federal government trampled on the rights of individuals, "it's possible that there might have to be some" backlash. The speech was televised, and Brandenburg was convicted of violating Ohio law.

The Supreme Court disagreed because Brandenburg had not incited any *imminent* violence, but had merely made vague statements about what might be possible at some unspecified time in the future. As Trevor Timm, co-founder and the executive director of the Freedom of the Press Foundation, has noted,

> [T]he Supreme Court's decision in *Brandenburg v. Ohio* effectively overturned Schenck and any authority the case still carried. There, the Court held that inflammatory speech—and even speech advocating violence by members of the Ku Klux Klan—is protected under the First Amendment, unless the speech "is directed to inciting or producing imminent lawless action and is likely to incite or produce such action." (Timm, 2012)

The irony is, therefore, that many people cite Holmes's words approvingly, unaware that they appeared in a case that restricted an individual's right to protest against the government in wartime, while ignoring the fact that that ruling was overturned in a later case that defended the rights of the Ku Klux Klan.

Moreover, other Supreme Court rulings are also relevant for the understanding of how case law has refined, expanded, and occasionally limited the First Amendment's right of free speech.

- In *Gitlow v. New York*, 268 US 652 (1925), the Supreme Court ruled that the Fourteenth Amendment extended the First Amendment's protections of free speech not only to individuals but also to state governments.

- In *Chaplinsky v. New Hampshire*, 315 US 568 (1942), the Supreme Court clarified that "fighting words" are not protected by the First Amendment because they do not "express ideas" or have "high social value."
- In *West Virginia State Board of Education v. Barnette*, 319 US 624 (1943), the Supreme Court held that state laws compelling students to salute the American flag or say the Pledge of Allegiance in public schools were unconstitutional.
- In the *United States v. O'Brien*, 391 US 367 (1968), the Supreme Court ruled that a law forbidding people from burning their draft cards did not violate the First Amendment's protection of free speech.
- In *Tinker v. Des Moines Independent Community School District*, 393 US 503 (1969), the Supreme Court established that armbands worn by students to protest a war could not be forbidden in public schools because they did not pass the test of causing a "substantial disruption" to the school's activities.
- In *Cohen v. California*, 403 US 15 (1971), the Supreme Court ruled that free speech cannot be restricted merely because it is offensive or contains language that others may find offensive.
- In *Texas v. Johnson*, 491 US 397 (1989), the Supreme Court declared that state laws prohibiting desecration of the American flag were unconstitutional.
- In *RAV v. City of St. Paul*, 505 US 377 (1992), the Supreme Court over-turned a local ordinance banning racially motivated political speech.
- In *Virginia v. Black*, 538 US 343 (2003), the Supreme Court ruled that cross burnings could be banned if they were intended to intimidate others but could not be banned if they were performed merely as acts of political speech.
- In *Garcetti v. Ceballos*, 547 US 410 (2006), the Supreme Court decided that, when government employees make statements pursuant to their position as public employees rather than as private citizens, their speech has no First Amendment protection.
- In *Morse v. Frederick*, 551 US 393 (2007), the Supreme Court established that the right of a public school to discourage drug use outweighed the right of students to promote drug use.
- In *Holder v. Humanitarian Law Project*, 561 US 1 (2010), the Supreme Court ruled that, under the USA PATRIOT Act, individuals and groups could be prevented from providing training or literature to foreign terrorist organizations, even if that training or literature was designed for constructive purposes such as teaching the organization how to resolve conflicts peacefully.

- In *Citizens United v. Federal Election Commission*, 558 US 310 (2010), the Supreme Court decided that the free speech clause of the First Amendment prohibits the government from restricting payments for political communications, not just by individuals, but also by corporations and nonprofit organizations.
- In *Lane v. Franks*, 573 US 228 (2014), the Supreme Court declared that the First Amendment protects public employees who are compelled to provide truthful testimony in court pursuant to a subpoena.

By publicizing these cases, colleges and universities have an opportunity to promote greater understanding of what the right of free speech does and does not entail in a number of different ways. First, federal case law in the United States makes it clear that freedom of speech is an evolving concept. Public standards of acceptable behavior change. New forms of media emerge. And legal challenges sometimes cause earlier decisions to be refined or overturned entirely. What *free speech* meant in 1919 when the Schenck case was decided wasn't exactly the same thing as in 2014 when *Lane v. Franks* was decided. Further changes can be expected in the future.

Second, students (and sometimes members of the faculty and administration as well) don't always understand the difference between a *circuit court* ruling and a *Supreme Court ruling*. For example, in 2020, the 9th US Circuit Court of Appeals (case number 18-15712) ruled against Prager University, a nonaccredited institution that produces political videos, in its claim that YouTube "performs a public function" and thus could not restrict access to its videos through age limits. But until such time that this case is appealed to the US Supreme Court, if it ever is and if the court accepts the case, then the Prager ruling establishes a precedent only for the 9th US Circuit (covering a large section of the western United States), not for the country as a whole. In other words, the decision of a court has precedent value only within the court's territorial jurisdiction.

Third, the concept of free speech can vary widely from country to country. Despite efforts to promote globalism and an international mindset at American colleges and universities, many students (and again some faculty members and administrators as well) in the United States tend to be Americentric in their outlook. The Irish constitution, for example, protects free speech but also notes that speech that undermines "public order or morality or the authority of the State" can be restricted. In a similar way, Australia's constitution does protect political speech but does not explicitly extend that freedom to other domains. Laws in the United Kingdom permit prior restraint of speech and approach concepts like libel very differently from laws in the United States.

For this reason, institutions of higher education have an opportunity as well as a responsibility to clarify for their stakeholders the element of *context* in matters involving free speech. *Where* something is said, *when* it is said, and *how* it is said can determine whether a communication is protected. Although "shouting 'Fire!' in a crowded theater" is a highly imperfect example of how the context of speech functions, it remains a common segue into these discussions for many people because it is such a familiar expression.

UNDERSTANDING THE IMPORTANCE OF CIVILITY

In 2011, while speaking about a new civics initiative at the National Press Club, the actor Richard Dreyfuss was asked about the nature of a civil society. He responded as follows.

> Civility is not not saying negative or harsh things. It is not the absence of critical analysis. It is the manner in which we are sharing this territorial freedom of political discussion. If our discourse is yelled and screamed and interrupted and patronized, that's uncivil. I don't care what the issue is and I don't care who the people and the players are. (Ballasy, 2011)

Dreyfuss's answer contains several important observations relative to the sort of civil interactions that are a goal at most colleges and universities.

First, civility consists of more than simply refraining from incivility. Dreyfuss's double negative (*not not*) suggests that being civil means more than avoidance of abusive words or actions. It means taking positive steps to help a society—or your own small corner of society—become a place where people are respected and where differences of opinions are approached constructively.

Second, a civil society (or a civil campus) isn't one where critical thinking goes out the window. As the philosopher Peter Kreeft has said, "Be egalitarian regarding persons. Be elitist regarding ideas" (Kreeft, 2016).

> Gresham's Law in economics states that "bad money drives out good." But a type of Reverse Gresham's Law applies to higher education: good ideas drive out bad ideas. As the Supreme Court Justice Louis D. Brandeis established in the case of *Whitney v. California*, "If there be time to expose through discussion, the falsehoods and fallacies, to avert the evil by the processes of education, the remedy to be applied is more speech, not enforced silence" (*Whitney v. California*, 274 US 357 1927). In other words, the solution to "bad speech" is not less speech but more. (Cipriano and Buller, 2020)

But countering ideas in a civil manner involves rejecting the message while respecting the messenger. That's not just politeness for the sake of politeness. That's actually effective argumentation. If you treat people with rudeness or contempt, they stop listening to your message. If you treat them civilly, they may actually listen to what you're saying.

Third, civility means not picking and choosing whom to treat with respect. You don't create a civil society only by demonstrating respect to those who agree with you. This lesson is one that every faculty member at a college or university should understand. When their students engage in logical inconsistencies or misinterpret the available evidence, they don't treat those students with contempt; they approach the situation as an opportunity to do their jobs as teachers.

Very few professors today take as their role model the harsh and derisive Professor Kingsfield played by John Houseman in the movie *The Paper Chase* (Twentieth Century-Fox Film Corporation, 1973). So, why do some of them engage with nonstudents that way? They're missing the opportunity for a teachable moment by forgetting one of their primary responsibilities as a faculty member: to convey wisdom to others.

UNDERSTANDING THE IMPORTANCE OF COLLEGIALITY

People sometimes speak about civility and collegiality as though they were the same thing. They're not. Someone can be civil to you by greeting you as the two of you pass in the hallway and never saying an unkind word to you. But if that person increases your workload by never "stepping up to the plate" when needed, following through on commitments, or meeting deadlines, is that person really acting like a colleague?

Collegiality is one of those qualities that's often easier to identify when it's absent than when it's present. Almost everyone can point to behavior that constitutes a clear lack of collegiality, but it can be difficult to think of examples of ordinary, day-to-day actions that can be characterized as collegial. That's why different researchers seem to approach academic collegiality in different ways. Here are a few examples.

> *Collegiality* refers to opportunities for faculty members to feel that they belong to a mutually respected community of scholars who value each faculty member's contribution to the institution and feel concern for their colleagues' well-being. (Gappa, Austin, and Trice, 2007, 305)

Collegiality means cooperative interaction among colleagues . . . [and] collective responsibility shared by each member of a group of colleagues with minimal supervision from above. (Cipriano, 2011, 15)

Collegiality is not simply a matter of being nice to the people we work with. It consists of behaving in an appropriately professional manner that promotes, to the greatest extent possible, the primary functions of our institutions, including teaching, scholarship, and service. (Buller, 2012, 218)

These definitions illustrate six different components of collegiality in an academic setting.

First, collegiality is about being part of a community. Every profession probably has its own sense of community among those who engage in it, but for college professors, as for people in the military, this sense is particularly strong. Faculty members often speak about the community of scholars, debate and sometimes argue about whether an administrator is a member of the *corps of instruction*, and view themselves as part of an enterprise that unites them, regardless of the specific institution they serve.

Second, collegiality is about mutual respect. Earlier it was noted that respect is an important aspect of civility. But note one important addition here: collegiality involves *mutual* respect. You can respect someone regardless of any power differential that may exist between the two of you. Professors respect their students not in the sense that they necessarily defer to them but in the sense that they recognize they have rights and deserve to be treated with dignity.

Collegiality is, however, more than the sort of respect you might show anyone. It implies the sort of respect shared among equals or peers. The very words *colleague* and *collegiality* imply this sense of mutuality. The Latin prefix *col-* (*con-*, *cum*) means *with* or *together*, as in the English verb *collect*. The Latin verb *legare* means *to entrust* or *to deputize*, as in the English verb *delegate.* Colleagues are people who share a task entrusted to them. It becomes far more difficult to perform that shared task if mutual respect breaks down among those who have been deputized to perform it.

Third, collegiality involves concern for the well-being of one's coworkers. You can be civil to someone you pass on the street, but not even think of that person's well-being. But you can't do that if you're sincerely someone's colleague. That person's welfare matters to you. You care about his or her health, safety, professional success, and happiness. As soon as you stop caring about those things, you cease being the person's colleague and become merely a co-worker.

Fourth, collegiality requires a shared sense of responsibility. That person mentioned earlier who was civil to you but wasn't willing to accept his or her share of your program's responsibilities wasn't really acting like a colleague. Colleagues don't have time for a "that's not my job" mentality. They understand that everyone in higher education has to do things not in the job description if the work of the unit is going to be done. So, colleagues "step up" when asked. Even better, they step up *before* they're asked.

Fifth, colleagues don't work for the good of their programs merely because their bosses are watching them. They hold one another accountable. In fact, they hold *themselves* accountable. Unlike the type of employee who shows up for work only to receive a paycheck, colleagues are dedicated to what they do and to one another. They see themselves as part of an important enterprise and thus often put in long hours that go far beyond the typical work day.

Sixth, collegiality, even when it's not demanded by one's contract or the faculty handbook, is an assumed requirement for employment as a professor. In a landmark decision for the Fourth US circuit, it was established that collegiality is a valid criterion in tenure decisions alongside such widely accepted criteria as teaching, scholarship, and service (*Mayberry v. Dees*, 663 F.2d 502, 4th Cir. Ct. 1981).

Moreover, the Maryland court of appeals ruled that collegiality may be considered when personnel decisions are being made even if an institution's governance documents do not expressly cite collegiality as a distinct criterion (*University of Baltimore v. Iz*, 716 A.2d 1107, Md. Ct. App., 1998). In other words, collegiality is such an integral part of being a college professor that it is regarded as a requirement for the job *even if a college or university never mentions it*. Most faculty handbooks don't mention that you actually have to show up for work and can't house your family in a classroom, but those are requirements of employment, too. They're simply assumed.

These six aspects of collegiality in higher education are important because of the distinctive organizational culture found at colleges and universities. In a hierarchical organization, such as that found in the military and at many corporations, decisions are made at upper levels of the unit, with lower levels mostly consigned to implementing decisions made by others. But even though the organizational charts of most institutions of higher education look hierarchical on paper, they actually don't function that way when it comes to the way in which many decisions are made.

For example, curricular decisions aren't initiated by the governing board, president, or chancellor. They're initiated by faculty members who act either individually or as part of small groups. Similarly, promotion decisions don't start with the upper levels of the institutional hierarchy. They start with applications made by individual faculty members. Curricular proposals, promotion applications, and similar matters involving the faculty thus move from the "bottom" of the organizational pyramid to the "top."

Hierarchies aren't supposed to function that way. The reason why so many decision-making processes operate as they do is that, in many ways, colleges and universities aren't perfect hierarchies. They may be *social* hierarchies, with faculty feeling that they're somehow superior to the staff and full professors feeling that they're superior to instructors, but when it comes to decision-making processes, democracy and consensus-building take precedence. (On higher education's decision-making procedures, see Buller and Reeves, 2018, 33–37.)

Consider how many decisions are made by committees, task forces, and other groups in higher education. Whenever possible, these bodies try to achieve consensus. When consensus isn't possible, votes are typically taken. But regardless of whether the decision is made by consensus or majority vote, there is usually a (sometimes quite lengthy) discussion and debate before that occurs. And for discussion and debate to be effective, there must be collegiality.

Anyone who has ever witnessed a faculty meeting knows that faculty interactions can often become quite heated. In these situations, collegiality is sometimes more an ideal than a reflection of reality. Nevertheless, the fact remains that the essential features of collegiality—a sense of community, a striving for mutual respect, concern for the well-being of others, shared responsibility, commitment to the task even when not so ordered by one's supervisor, and willingness to go above and beyond the requirements of the policy manual—are necessary for committee work.

To put it bluntly, without committees very little would ever get done in higher education. And committees require a dedication to collegiality even when that dedication is a goal not always reached.

UNDERSTANDING THE NATURE OF PROTEST

At the beginning of Chapter 2, it was noted that the history of higher education in the west was marked by protest from the very beginning. But what actually *is* a protest? Etymologically, a protest is a public declaration, since the term is derived from the Latin prefix *pro-* meaning *out in front of* or *publicly* (as in the English word *promote*, "to move out in front") and the deponent verb *testari* meaning *to assert* or *bear witness* (as in the English word *attestation*, "witness or evidence that is given to an allegation").

The Christian group known as the Protestants thus receive their name both because the founders of this movement bore public witness to a set of beliefs and because they protested against the 1526 decision of the Holy Roman Emperor Charles V to enforce an edict condemning Martin Luther and his teachings regardless of the local ruler's beliefs. A protest is thus, at least traditionally, two things simultaneously: a condemnation of an existing policy and a statement of support for an alternative policy.

A protest is also different in one respect from a demonstration, which may oppose a given policy without proposing a specific alternative (e.g., demonstrating against a war without recommending a clear path to peace), or a mass meeting, which may recommend a plan for the future without opposing an existing or proposed policy (e.g., holding a mass meeting to demand that a new federal department be created).

Because of this difference, protests in the United States are protected under the First Amendment, which, as noted earlier, gives people the right "to petition the Government for a redress of grievances." Redressing grievances inevitably involves objection to a current policy or action while proposing a new one. In a similar way, demonstrations and mass meetings are protected under the First Amendment's guarantee of the right "peaceably to assemble."

But just as the US courts have decided that free speech and academic freedom are rights, but not rights that always exist without restrictions, so is the right to protest subject at times to restrictions. The most important of these restrictions is the so-called *time, place, and manner restriction*, established by *Grayned v. City of Rockford* (408 US 104, 92 S. Ct. 2294 [1972]). Affirming the right of a city to impose an antinoise ordinance against a group picketing in front of a school, the Supreme Court ruled that people do have a right to protest but that right does not allow them to interrupt activities for the general welfare of the public.

For example, a protest cannot block an ambulance transporting a critically ill patient to a hospital. To support the right of protesters but not place a burden on the public, government entities can impose three types of restrictions on protests.

- Time. *When* a protest occurs can be restricted. For example, it cannot interfere with the rights of students to learn during the regular school day.
- Place. *Where* a protest occurs can be restricted. For example, it cannot occur in a state capital if it prevents legislators from meeting.
- Manner. *How* a protest occurs can be restricted. For example, it cannot consist of signs or banners of such a size that they violate other legal ordinances.

Other court cases have clarified how these rights and restrictions are to be balanced.

- *Chicago Police Dept. v. Mosley* (408 US 92 [1972]) clarified that protests *can* occur on school property if they have a legitimate relevance to school activities, such as a labor protest by the teachers themselves.
- *Heffron v. International Society for Krishna Consciousness, Inc.* (452 US 640 [1981]) ruled that valid time, place, and manner restrictions permitted a state to confine the sale and distribution of literature by religious organizations to an assigned location at a state fair, as long as the restriction applied to all religious groups equally.
- *Clark v. Community for Creative Non-Violence* (468 US 288 [1982]) upheld the right of the National Park Service to prevent protesters from sleeping in Lafayette Mall and the National Mall in Washington, DC, to draw attention to the plight of the homeless because there were other parks where sleeping was permitted and the restriction at the two sites named in the dispute supported a valid interest in maintaining the condition of national parks.
- *Ward v. Rock Against Racism* (491 US 781 [1989]) established a three-pronged test for restrictions on the right to protest. Restrictions have to be *content neutral* (i.e., they may not favor any one side in a dispute), *narrowly tailored to serve a significant governmental interest* (i.e., they must specify precisely what goal they seek to achieve and that goal must be important), and *open to alternative channels for protest* (i.e., they must not be so restrictive as to make protest all but impossible).
- *Madsen v. Women's Health Center, Inc.* (512 US 753 [1994]) held that a clinic could prevent antiabortion demonstrators from blocking its entrance as long as restrictions were not imposed more broadly than necessary to protect the state's interests in promoting free access to commerce and health care.
- *Hill v. Colorado* (530 US 703 [2000]) reaffirmed the right of a clinic to limit protest, education, distribution of literature, or counseling within eight feet of its entrance so that patients would have free access to the clinic.

Students and faculty members who wish to engage in a protest are sometimes unaware that time, place, and manner restrictions exist. At the same time, these restrictions are often imposed by colleges and universities in a way that some observers believe go far beyond their legal justification.

The Foundation of Individual Rights in Education (FIRE) is an organization supporting free speech rights throughout the higher education community that has received funding from a number of conservative groups, including the Charles G. Koch Foundation, the Adolph Coors Foundation, and the Searle Freedom Trust. With its more conservative perspective, FIRE has clashed with more liberal organizations like the AAUP over several issues, such as the desirability of campus "free speech bills," initiatives that are intended to defend against what FIRE regards as widespread attacks on the open exchange of ideas in higher education. (See Campus Free-Speech Legislation: History, Progress, and Problems, n.d.)

Samantha Harris, FIRE's vice president for procedural advocacy has been particularly critical of time, place, and manner restrictions, arguing,

> Public universities often try to justify restrictive demonstration policies by arguing that they are "reasonable time, place, and manner" regulations, which are permissible under First Amendment law. . . . So, for example, a university might establish regulations preventing demonstrations from interfering with pedestrian or vehicular traffic or place restrictions on the use of amplified sound so that expressive activities do not interfere with classes in progress. Those are reasonable, content-neutral provisions that serve a significant governmental interest (i.e., keeping traffic flowing or allowing classes to continue) while still allowing speakers other means to spread their message. Too many universities, however, mistake a narrow exception as *carte blanche* to regulate student demonstrations. Regulations that limit free speech to just one or two areas of campus or require prior administrative approval for all expressive activity are not reasonable time, place, and manner regulations. (Harris, 2012)

Moreover, state legislatures have increasingly created additional restrictions on the right to protest. As a study conducted by PEN America, an organization whose acronym once stood for Poets, Essayists, Novelists in America and that is dedicated to the right of free expression, has concluded,

> [I]n 2015 and 2016, . . . bills that would restrict or otherwise criminalize demonstrations were introduced just six times and none became law. But after the 2016 election, the number of anti-protest proposals ballooned to 56 in 2017, 17 in 2018, and 37 in 2019—23 eventually became law over the course of those three years. Most of these bills heighten penalties for protesters who demonstrate near critical-infrastructure sites, march on public roadways, or otherwise engage in conduct that law-enforcement officials deem "unlawful." Some require protesters to pay for law-enforcement time, others shield officers from liability if they harm protesters, and still others criminalize mask-wearing. (Benavidez, 2020)

Because some institutions of higher education, particularly research universities, include facilities that may be regarded as "critical-infrastructure sites," these laws may come into direct conflict with the right to protest that has traditionally been celebrated at public universities. The result is that academic leaders sometimes face a dilemma: which do you uphold, the law or the principles that your profession has cherished for centuries?

A second dilemma that many academic leaders face is that, as illustrated previously, while a person's right to protest is not unlimited, neither is a public university's right to impose time, place, and manner restrictions. Protests sometimes arise spontaneously because of current events. The primary function of a college or university is the creation and transmission of knowledge, and protests can be "living laboratories" where knowledge is created and transmitted.

Thus, the teachable moment that institutions of higher education have consists of helping members of their community better understand where the right to protest begins—and where it ends. But that mission must always be coupled with helping members of the higher education community better understand where time, place, and manner restrictions begin—and where they end.

UNDERSTANDING THE NATURE OF TRIGGER WARNINGS

As was seen in Chapter 1, the concept of *trigger warnings* often gets lumped in with the topic of free speech because some people see these warnings as unwanted restrictions on speech. By alerting students that sensitive or controversial topics are about to be discussed (and often giving them an opportunity to remove themselves from these discussions), trigger warnings are sometimes seen as a dereliction of a faculty member's responsibility to challenge students even if certain issues make them uncomfortable.

The AAUP even calls trigger warnings a "current threat to academic freedom in the classroom," arguing,

> The presumption that students need to be protected rather than challenged in a classroom is at once infantilizing and anti-intellectual. It makes comfort a higher priority than intellectual engagement and . . . it singles out politically controversial topics like sex, race, class, capitalism, and colonialism for attention. Indeed, if such topics are associated with triggers, correctly or not, they are likely to be marginalized if not avoided altogether by faculty who fear complaints for offending or discomforting some of their students. Although all faculty are affected by potential charges of this kind, non-tenured and contingent faculty are particularly at risk. In this way the demand for trigger warnings creates a repressive, "chilly climate" for critical thinking in the classroom. (On Trigger Warnings, 2014)

On the other hand, many professors and administrators defend the use of trigger warnings, claiming that they enhance rather than restrict free speech. The highly diverse student body of the modern university includes many who suffer from some sort of trauma, such as sexual abuse or combat experiences leading to PTSD. By alerting students that images or graphic descriptions of events that can lead to trauma will be encountered in a course or lesson, trigger warnings improve the educational experience of these students by giving them a free choice about whether they are currently ready to relive and discuss traumatic events. Trigger warnings, in other words, are just another way in which colleges and universities try to be inclusive by meeting the individual needs of a no longer homogeneous student population.

Research on the effectiveness of trigger warnings is mixed at best. One study published in the journal *Clinical Psychological Science* found that, in terms of protecting vulnerable students from experiences that might negatively affect their educations, trigger warnings weren't particularly helpful or harmful (Sanson, Strange, and Garry, 2019). Perhaps predictably, that result may be interpreted as "the glass is half empty" by those inclined to disparage the use of trigger warnings ("They don't help!") and "the glass is half full" by those who support them ("Since they don't do harm, why not at least try them?").

Another study suggested that trigger warnings are indeed harmful because they reinforce people's views of themselves as victims, as defined solely by their traumas and not by the totality of their life experiences. (Jones, Bellet, and McNally, 2020). Yet when counselors at colleges and universities were asked about the potential benefit of trigger warnings, their view was very different.

> Counselors . . . may have a different viewpoint from other academic leaders regarding trigger warnings, as counselors directly serve students and help them to address their mental health needs. In fact, trigger warnings and safe spaces may serve a functional purpose in today's college campuses, and the pushback may stem from a fundamental misunderstanding of the purpose of trigger warnings. Some administrators subscribe to the belief that trigger warnings prevent individuals from grappling with difficult or uncomfortable materials, but Elana Newman, PhD, research director for the Dart Center for Journalism and Trauma and professor at the University of Tulsa, argues that triggering material isn't simply something that might offend students. "Being [made] uncomfortable by topics or values or things that upset you is very different than having a symptomatic mental health response," says Newman. (Wake Forest University n.d.)

Since this issue is so divisive, how can colleges and universities help students and the public understand why they do or don't encourage trigger warnings in a clear and effective manner? One approach schools might consider taking is to begin with the observation that trigger warnings aren't a phenomenon that's limited to higher education. The general public is exposed to them all the time. Movie ratings like G, PG, are PG-13 are, in their own way, a type of trigger warning, as are the announcements that "viewer discretion is advised" before a television program or "the following story contains images that may be inappropriate for some viewers" before a news report. This type of notices alerts viewers to what they're about to see, *giving them the choice* either to prepare themselves for content that may be difficult or, if they decide that the material would have negative consequences for them, to opt out of seeing it.

The real issue question on college campuses is thus: are college professors *required* to issue trigger warnings or are they merely *allowed* to do so? If they are compelled to issue trigger warnings in their courses, then there might be a valid concern that an individual faculty member's academic freedom is being curtailed. But if professors are merely allowed to offer trigger warnings, based on their own professional discretion, then banning them can be seen as an equal infringement.

This distinction isn't sufficient for the AAUP, however. It argues,

> There are reasons . . . for concern that even voluntary use of trigger warnings included on syllabi may be counterproductive to the educational experience. Such trigger warnings conflate exceptional individual experience of trauma with the anticipation of trauma for an entire group, and assume that individuals will respond negatively to certain content. A trigger warning might lead a student to simply not read an assignment or it might elicit a response from students they otherwise would not have had, focusing them on one aspect of a text and thus precluding other reactions. . . . Instead of putting the onus for avoiding such responses on the teacher, cases of serious trauma should be referred to student health services. Faculty should, of course, be sensitive that such reactions may occur in their classrooms, but they should not be held responsible for them. (On Trigger Warnings, 2014)

Nevertheless, banning a widely used educational practice entirely because it "*might* lead a student to simply not read an assignment" is not a particularly compelling argument, nor is letting faculty members decide the issue for themselves "putting the onus" on them or holding them "responsible" for negative reactions.

It would be far more in the interest of academic freedom (not to mention free speech) to allow a faculty member to issue alerts to students that sensitive material is likely to be covered in a particular course or unit if the faculty member regards such an alert as appropriate. Understanding the nature of trigger warnings that includes both their rationale and the students' suggestion that their value is limited can thus become a teachable moment for all constituencies of a college or university.

HOW TO TAKE ADVANTAGE OF THE TEACHABLE MOMENT

Helping members of the campus community better understand concepts like academic freedoms, freedom of speech, civility, collegiality, and the right to protest—as well as legal limits to these freedoms and rights—can be a valuable part of any school's mission. But how do you promote this understanding in a way that's effective?

One strategy that some colleges and universities have adopted is to create a website dedicated to these issues. Perhaps the best example of this approach is the Free Speech and the First Amendment website developed by North Carolina State University (NC State) (Free Speech, 2020). This resource answers such questions as, "Which types of speech are not protected by the First Amendment?," "Are nonverbal symbols, such as swastikas or burning flags, constitutionally protected?," and "Can people who oppose a speaker's message use their own freedom of speech to shout down that speaker's message?" It also addresses issues where federal law and institution policy intersect, such as how time, place, and manner restrictions are applied at the university, the proper way to protest a policy or event on campus, and what to do if a student believes that constitutional rights or the systems policies on free speech are being infringed.

The NC State website also includes links to relevant university policies, case law on free speech and the right to protest, and resources for further study. The way in which information is presented on the website makes it clear that having all members of the community both *know about* constitutional rights and feel free to *exercise* those constitutional rights is an appropriate goal for the university. It's thus a superb example of how to transform a potentially divisive issue into a teachable moment.

Other good models for educational websites include the Free Speech at UT: Frequently Asked Questions page developed by the University of Tennessee Knoxville (Free Speech at UT, n.d.), the Free Expression page developed by the University of Colorado Boulder (Free Expression, n.d.), and the Free Speech on Campus page developed by the University of California at Los Angeles (Free Speech on Campus, 2020). While these websites are a little more difficult to navigate than NC State's, they do provide critical information about such topics as what crosses the line of unprotected speech, how the institution educates its students about free speech issues, the school's approach to student activism, and how professors can deal with challenges arising in their classrooms.

A second strategy commonly adopted by colleges and universities is to take advantage of the federal holiday known as Constitution Day as a means of promoting campus dialogue on the topic of free speech and campus civility.

In the wake of the events occurring on September 11, 2001, the United States Congress included a provision in its omnibus spending bill in May of 2005 that any school, including colleges and universities, receiving federal funds had to create annual events celebrating the signing of the US Constitution on September 17, 1787. Because the phrase "institutions receiving federal funds" includes all schools where students are eligible for federal loans, the Constitution Day requirement applies to nearly all colleges and universities, public and private, in the Unites States.

When the law was first adopted, many professors regarded the Constitution Day requirement as an undesirable attempt by the federal government to mandate patriotism in higher education. And because mandating any specific belief or ideology seemed to many faculty members to be itself unconstitutional, the very concept of a required Constitution Day struck them as paradoxical. But the focus of the law was not to demand *reverence* for the Constitution (even though many of the legislators voting for the bill hoped that might be a useful byproduct of the law) but rather to require *educational activities* concerning the Constitution. And the precise nature of those activities was left up to the institution.

For this reason, many schools have used the annual Constitution Day to educate students and the community about free speech issues. For example, in 2018, the University of Hawai'i at Mānoa dedicated a substantial portion of Constitution Day to presentations and discussions that dealt with the topic of free speech on campus (Hiraishi, 2018). That topic was particularly relevant to the university because, earlier that year, it had received notification from FIRE that it had "at least one policy that both clearly and substantially restricts freedom of speech" (Carroll, 2018). Four years earlier the school had been criticized for applying time, place, and manner restrictions in an excessively limiting manner. Two students had even been instructed not to distribute copies of the US Constitution outside the university's sole "free speech zone."

In 2017, the educational program for Constitution Day at Trinity Washington University in Washington, DC, included a poll of faculty and students on matters related to free speech. 67.93 percent of the faculty and staff agreed or strongly agreed with the statement "I believe that freedom of speech should be absolute at all times and in all places," while 79.6 percent of students agreed or strongly agreed with that statement. Among faculty and staff, 50.98 percent either agreed or strongly agreed that the government could limit freedom of speech "for good reasons," while only 43.75 percent of students agreed or strongly agreed with that statement (President's Blog, 2017). Celebrating free speech on Constitution Day in a very different manner, Vanderbilt University in 2019 hosted a number of entertainment events, including a concert of songs that had been banned in the past (Vanderbilt News, 2020).

There is no one way to make the issues involving free speech and campus civility a teachable event at all colleges and universities. The important thing is for institutions to choose a format that suits their mission, tradition, and needs. Campuses might consider disseminating the quiz on free speech and campus civility that appeared in the first chapter of this book. They might conduct panel discussions on such topics as:

- Were those who protested in 2020 for reopening the US economy more quickly during the COVID-19 pandemic exercising their valid rights of free speech or endangering the public?
- Given that the US Supreme Court has repeatedly ruled that restrictions may apply to the First Amendment right of free speech, what restrictions (if any) should apply to the First Amendment right of free speech?
- Again, given that the US Supreme Court has repeatedly ruled that restrictions may apply to the First Amendment right of free speech, what restrictions (if any) should apply to the Second Amendment right to bear arms?
- What new challenges to the right of free speech are created by technologies that had not yet been invented when the US Constitution was ratified?
- Is there such a thing as a right to (or an obligation for) civility and, if so, how is that right affected by the constitutional right of free speech?

CONCLUSION

Issues of free speech, academic freedom, and the right to protest are so interwoven with the concept of higher education that many professors and administrators find it difficult to separate them. Nostalgia for the "quiet, respectful campuses of the past" usually stems from a romantic notion that had little basis in reality. Colleges and universities have always been places where challenging concepts have not only been developed and disseminated; they have also been practiced, at times quite loudly.

Despite this heritage, however, colleges and universities remain places where not everyone understands what terms like *academic freedom* and *collegiality* mean. Faculty members and academic leaders thus have an opportunity, regardless of their specialties, to teach students *and one another* about existing laws and existing policies, as well as existing injustices. There remains a teachable moment in the area of free speech and campus civility for those with enough courage in their convictions to pursue it.

KEY POINTS IN THIS CHAPTER

- The expressions *academic freedom*, *freedom of speech*, *civility*, and *collegiality* are used broadly even though many people in academic life don't fully understand their background, implication, or legal frameworks.
- The solution to "bad speech" is not less speech but more.
- In the United States, there is a growing gap between liberals and conservatives on many social issues. Colleges and universities can play an important role in helping to close that gap.
- Individual academic freedom is based on the premise that scholars should be free to discuss and conduct research within their areas of specialty. One of the safeguards of that right is the process of course syllabus review by peers to ensure that the content of the course meets and is relevant to appropriate professional standards.
- The Pickering Balancing Test is one useful device that can balance a faculty member's academic freedom and free speech rights with a public university's right to pursue its mission in an orderly and civil fashion.
- Many people misunderstand the origins and implications of the phrase "You can't shout "Fire!' in a crowded theater" or how that limitation of free speech in the United States was modified by later case law.
- Civility involves more than avoidance of abusive words or actions. It also includes a willingness to take positive steps that demonstrate respect to other people.
- Collegiality among the professoriate goes beyond mere civility to include assuming one's fair share of professional responsibilities. Even when collegiality is not specifically required by one's contract, it is an assumed requirement for employment as a faculty member.
- Protests are different from demonstrations (which may oppose positions or policies without proposing specific alternatives) or mass meetings (which may recommend actions without opposing current positions or policies). In the United States, the right to protest is thus protected under the "redress of grievances" clause of the First Amendment.
- Colleges and universities may impose time, place, and manner restrictions on protests but those restrictions must be reasonable. They must be based on a valid need to protect the institution's right to fulfill its mission and must offer adequate alternatives.
- Teaching a campus community about free speech and civility can include such approaches as designing a thorough, easily navigated website devoted to these topics and, in the United States, taking advantage of the Constitution Day requirement to promote educational events dealing with free speech.

QUESTIONS FOR REFLECTION

1. Given that courts in the United States have consistently ruled that reasonable, narrowly tailored restrictions can be imposed on the First Amendment right of free speech, would you similarly support reasonable, narrowly tailored restrictions on:
   a. The First Amendment right to freedom of religion?
   b. The First Amendment right to freedom of the press?
   c. The Second Amendment right to bear arms?
   d. The Fifth Amendment right against seizure of property?
   e. The Sixth Amendment right to confront one's accusers?
   Why or why not would you support these restrictions? If you would support reasonable, narrowly tailored restrictions, what would they be? How might the Ninth Amendment (which guarantees that rights provided by the Constitution may not infringe on a person's other rights) impose "restrictions on these restrictions"?
2. The First Amendment to the US Constitution gives people the right *peaceably* to assemble. Does that phrasing, in your opinion, constitute an obligation for civility?
3. Martin Luther King, Jr. (1929–1968) is frequently cited as an advocate for peaceful protest and nonviolent opposition. Nevertheless, in his *Letter from a Birmingham Jail*, he wrote the following:

> I must confess that over the past few years I have been gravely disappointed with the white moderate. I have almost reached the regrettable conclusion that the Negro's great stumbling block in his stride toward freedom is not the White Citizen's Counciler or the Ku Klux Klanner, but the white moderate, who is more devoted to "order" than to justice; who prefers a negative peace which is the absence of tension to a positive peace which is the presence of justice; who constantly says: "I agree with you in the goal you seek, but I cannot agree with your methods of direct action"; who paternalistically believes he can set the timetable for another man's freedom; who lives by a mythical concept of time and who constantly advises the Negro to wait for a "more convenient season." Shallow understanding from people of good will is more frustrating than absolute misunderstanding from people of ill will. Lukewarm acceptance is much more bewildering than outright rejection. (King, 1963)

In your opinion, was King stating here that a desire for civility can at times become a barrier to progress? In a conflict between free speech and civility, are there ever circumstances under which a desire for civility becomes irrelevant? If so, what are those circumstances? If not, why is the obligation for civility of such paramount importance?

4. What is your position on trigger warnings? Are they useful tools to enhance the educational experience of students who have suffered from trauma? Are they unwarranted restrictions on the right of free speech by the professor or other students in the class? Is the truth somewhere in between?

REFERENCES

About the AAUP. (n.d.) https://www.aaup.org/about-aaup.

American Association of University Professors. (n.d.) 1940 statement of principles on academic freedom and tenure. https://www.aaup.org/report/1940-statement-princip les-academic-freedom-and-tenure.

Ballasy, N. (2011). MSNBC's Ed Schultz calling Dick Cheney an "enemy" of America "not uncivil," says civics initiative leader Richard Dreyfuss. *CNS News.* https://www.cnsnews.com/news/article/msnbc-s-ed-schultz-calling-dick-cheney-enemy -america-not-uncivil-says-civics-initiative.

Benavidez, N. (2020). First Amendment rights—if you agree with the president. *The Atlantic.* https://www.theatlantic.com/ideas/archive/2020/06/first-amendment -rightsif-you-agree-with-the-president/612211/?utm_source=feed.

Brandenburg v. Ohio: The Ohio Criminal Syndicalism Law. (2020). https://law.jrank .org/pages/23050/Brandenburg-v-Ohio-Ohio-Criminal-Syndicalism-Law.html.

Buller, J. (2012). *The essential department chair: A comprehensive desk reference* (second edition) San Francisco, CA: Wiley.

Buller, J. L., and Reeves, D. M. (2018). *The five cultures of academic development.* Washington, DC: CASE.

Campus Free-Speech Legislation: History, Progress, and Problems: AAUP. (n.d.). https://www.aaup.org/report/campus-free-speech-legislation-history-progress-and -problems.

Carroll, K. (2018). Code red to code yellow: University of Hawaii-Manoa updates its policies to earn a better free speech rating. *The Washington Examiner*. https://www .washingtonexaminer.com/red-alert-politics/code-red-to-code-yellow-university -of-hawaii-manoa-updates-its-policies-to-earn-a-better-free-speech-rating.

Cipriano, R. E. (2011). *Facilitating a collegial department in higher education: Strategies for success*. San Francisco: Jossey-Bass.

Cipriano, R. E, and Buller, J. L. (2020). Campus incivility and free speech: A contemporary dilemma. *Academic Leader*. https://www.academic-leader.com/topics/ institutional-culture/campus-incivility-and-free-speech-a-contemporary-dilemma.

Free Expression: University of Colorado Boulder. (n.d.). https://www.colorado.edu/ free-expression.

Free Speech at UT: Frequently Asked Questions. (n.d.). https://freespeech.utk.edu/ frequently-asked-questions/.

Free Speech on Campus: University of California at Los Angeles. (2020). https://equity.ucla.edu/know/freedom-of-speech/.

Free Speech: North Carolina State University. (2020). https://www.ncsu.edu/free-speech/.

Gappa, J. M., Austin, A. E., and Trice, A. G. *Rethinking faculty work: Higher education's strategic imperative*. San Francisco: Jossey-Bass.

Harris, S. (2012). Misunderstanding "time, place, and manner" restrictions. *FIRE Newsdesk*. https://www.thefire.org/misunderstanding-time-place-and-manner-restrictions/.

Hiraishi, K. (2018). Constitution Day discussion: Free speech on campus. *Hawai'i Public Radio*. https://www.hawaiipublicradio.org/post/constitution-day-discussion-free-speech-campus#stream/0.

Jones, P. J., Bellet, B. W., and McNally, R. J. (2020). Helping or harming? The effect of trigger warnings on individuals with trauma histories. *Clinical Psychological Science*. https://osf.io/axn6z/.

Kennedy, B., and Funk, C. (2019). Democrats and Republicans differ over role and value of scientists in policy debates. *Pew Research Center: Social and Demographic Trends*. https://www.pewresearch.org/fact-tank/2019/08/09/democrats-and-republicans-role-scientists-policy-debates/.

King, M. L. (1963). Letter from a Birmingham Jail. https://www.africa.upenn.edu/Articles_Gen/Letter_Birmingham.html.

Kreeft, P. (2016). https://twitter.com/ProfessorKreeft/status/727233811814187009?ref_src=twsrc%5Etfw.

National Archives Catalog. (1917). Act of June 15, 1917, Public Law 24 (Espionage Act), an act to punish acts of interference with the foreign relations, the neutrality, and the foreign commerce of the United States, to punish espionage, and better to enforce, the criminal laws of the United States, and for other purposes. https://catalog.archives.gov/id/5721240.

Oluwole, J. O. (2008). The Pickering Balancing test and public employment-free speech jurisprudence: The approaches of federal circuit courts of appeals. *Duquesne Law Review, 46*, 133–75.

On Trigger Warnings: The American Association of University Professors. https://www.aaup.org/report/trigger-warnings.

Parker, K. (2019). The growing partisan divide in views of higher education. *Pew Research Center: Social and Demographic Trends*. https://www.pewsocialtrends.org/essay/the-growing-partisan-divide-in-views-of-higher-education/.

President's Blog: Trinity Washington University. (2017). Constitution Day 2017: First Amendment poll, part one: Freedom of speech. https://www.trinitydc.edu/president/2017/09/constitution-day-2017-first-amendment-poll-part-one-freedom-of-speech/.

Protecting Academic Freedom: AAUP. (n.d.). https://www.aaup.org/our-work/protecting-academic-freedom.

Rainie, L., Keeter, S., and Perrin, A. (2019). Trust and distrust in America. *Pew Research Center: Social and Demographic Trends*. https://www.people-press.org/2019/07/22/trust-and-distrust-in-america/.

Sanson, M., Strange, D., and Garry, M. (2019). Trigger warnings are trivially helpful at reducing negative affect, intrusive thoughts, and avoidance. *Clinical Psychological Science, 7*(4), 778–93.

Timm, T. (2012). It's time to stop using the "fire in a crowded theater" quote. *The Atlantic*. https://www.theatlantic.com/national/archive/2012/11/its-time-to-stop-using-the-fire-in-a-crowded-theater-quote/264449/.

Twentieth Century-Fox Film Corporation. (1973). *The paper chase*. New York: Twentieth Century-Fox.

Vanderbilt News. (2020). Vanderbilt observes Constitution Day with free speech concert, voter registration, reading. https://news.vanderbilt.edu/2019/09/16/vanderbilt-observes-constitution-day-with-free-speech-concert-voter-registration-reading/.

Wake Forest University. (n.d.). Do "trigger warnings" on school campuses help? Counselors and students weigh in. https://counseling.online.wfu.edu/blog/do-trigger-warnings-on-school-campuses-help-counselors-and-students-weigh-in/.

RESOURCES

American Civil Liberties Association. (2020). Speech on campus. https://www.aclu.org/other/speech-campus.

Baer, U. (2019). *What snowflakes get right: Free speech, truth, and equality on campus*. New York: Oxford University Press.

Ben-Porath, S. R. (2017). *Free speech on campus*. Philadelphia: University of Pennsylvania Press.

Chemerinsky, E., and Gillman, H. (2018). *Free speech on campus*. New Haven, CT: Yale University Press.

Cose, E. (in press). *The Short life and curious death of free speech in America*. New York: HarperCollins.

Doyle, E. (2019). *Freedom of speech on campus*. New York: Greenhaven.

PEN America. (2020). Arresting dissent: Legislative restrictions on the right to protest. https://pen.org/wp-content/uploads/2020/05/Arresting-Dissent-FINAL.pdf.

Shiell, T. C. (2009). Campus hate speech on trial. (second edition) Lawrence: University Press of Kansas.

Slater, T. (2016). *Unsafe space: The crisis of free speech on campus*. London: Palgrave Macmillan.

Sun, J. C., and McClellan, G. S. (2020). *Student clashes on campus: A leadership guide to free speech*. New York: Routledge, Taylor and Francis.

Tee, V. (2003). *Free speech on campus: A legal review*. Horsham, PA: LRP.

Chapter Four

Preparing for Possible Scenarios

Problems sometimes become major crises largely because no one saw them coming. Or at least no one believed the people who *did* see them coming. The evidence suggesting that the attacks on September 11, 2001, would occur were ignored at the highest levels of government. The devastating effects of COVID-19 could have been reduced significantly if certain regions and nations had begun responding to it even one week earlier.

Crises in higher education are much the same. Some of the worst problems academic leaders have to deal with are those they simply didn't see coming. Emergency management specialists Mike Seymour and Simon Moore describe crises as either *cobras* or *pythons* (Seymour and Moore, 2000). A cobra is the type of crisis that strikes suddenly and without warning. A tornado rips through campus. An armed intruder invades a classroom. An explosion occurs in one of the labs.

A python creeps up on you more slowly. If you saw it was coming, you would have taken steps to avoid it or minimize its damage. But because the python lies unnoticed for too long, a disaster occurs. Unsustainable expenditures bring an institution to the brink of insolvency. Carelessness with research protocols become worse and worse until a major scandal occurs. A toxic faculty member is dismissed because people say, "Oh, that's just how he is," until he is tenured and causes a major personnel issue.

Problems that arise at colleges and university over a conflict between free speech and civility tend to be pythons that are mistaken for cobras. A protest over a speaker's remarks turns violent, and academic leaders feel that they had no way of preventing the resulting situation. "Well, we all know about the heckler's veto," they might say. "We can't cancel an event because we *suspect* there *might* be a problem. What could we have done? We had no way of knowing this crisis would occur."

Nevertheless, part of the reason why issues on college campuses get out of hand is that academic leaders devote too much time to planning and not enough to preparation. Colleges and universities trust in strategic planning—several accrediting bodies even *require* an institution to have a strategic plan—even though the sectors that developed this approach to implementing change, the military and the corporate world, have long since abandoned or at least questioned this practice. Strategic planning requires leaders to predict a future too far out to predict, and so many strategic plans end up being followed for only a year or two and then quietly abandoned. Or worse, they are simply superseded by another strategic plan.

The fact is that professionals in higher education are attracted to planning because it tries to impose a rational order on growth processes that frequently resist rational analysis. There are simply too many factors at play in the higher education environment to predict them all. Political, economic, social, climatic, technological, demographic, and other factors all interact with one another to change the higher education landscape dramatically.

Professors and administrators recognize this challenge for students but fail to see it in themselves. They understand that the twenty-year-old who has her entire career "planned out" for her is probably in for a rude awakening. She intends to have a premed major, go on to medical school followed by an internship, and then complete a residency. Afterward she'll start her own practice, get married, and have three children (two girls and a boy), while writing a novel in her spare time.

If "life planning" with that degree of specificity seems ridiculous, it's important to note that that same level of specificity is found in many strategic plans. Many schools fill their plans with metrics and targets (often to the exclusion of actual strategies for how to obtain them) that will soon become meaningless because the economic, political, and demographic environment in which the plan was conceived turns out to have been wholly different from the economic, political, and demographic environment in which the plan has to be carried out.

Our hypothetical student would have been better off if she'd engaged in a little less planning and a little more preparation. That premed major may not turn out to have been her best choice if she's not accepted into medical school or finds once she gets there that she really doesn't like this field. But the *preparations* she made in her life by learning the scientific method, understanding how to analyze a text, becoming proficient at critical thinking, recognizing historical patterns, and understanding the difference between correlation and causality will prepare her for a wide range of different futures. If an opportunity to work in a hospital in Paris suddenly "drops in her lap," the preparation she made by learning French enables her to take advantage of this unexpected development.

PREPARATION, FREE SPEECH, AND CIVILITY

In a similar way, colleges and universities are too often blindsided by crises involving free speech and civility because their focus has been on a specific plan, not general preparations. You can't plan for the armed intruder who's going to invade a classroom next Tuesday at 2:03 p.m., armed with three rifles and two pistols. But you can prepare for the eventuality of an active shooter scenario. Likewise, you can't plan for any specific speaker causing a specific kind of campus disturbance on a particular day, but you can prepare for it.

Scenario planning helps institutions prepare, not just for one possible future, but for many. Instead of assuming that the economy will progress in a certain way, a certain political party will control the legislature, and demographics will develop as predicted, scenario planning prepares for the most likely scenario but then asks, "Okay, but how would our strategy need to change if the economy turns out to be much worse than we're expecting in five years? How would we reinvest a budget surplus if the economy turns out to be much better than we're predicting? What would we do if we're facing a legislature that does everything it can to hinder our development? What would we do if laws were passed that were more to our benefit than current laws are?"

Imagining these different scenarios increases the likelihood that a school can be nimble enough to adapt its plans to suit changing circumstances. Even more importantly, however, scenario planning creates a *culture of preparation*. Simply by repeatedly thinking through various scenarios, the faculty, staff, and administration develop the skill to adjust their approaches when they receive new information. They also start making preparations that will enable them to respond to the "cobras" that strike suddenly, avoid the "pythons" that are sneaking up on them, and learn how to see situations in all their complexity.

Preparing for possible scenarios that deal with conflicts between free speech and civility can be a valuable exercise for all the stakeholders of an institution. Students can engage in this activity in a first-year seminar. Faculty members and administrators can engage in it as part of a development program. Board members can engage in it as part of their training. The hypothetical situations that are studied in a scenario exercise are unlikely to occur exactly as they're written, but they lead people to consider the best possible way of reacting in different situations. They also help people understand which skills they might need to develop now in case a challenge in the area of free speech and civility occurs at some point in the future.

EXERCISES FOR STUDENTS

Hypothetical case studies for students are useful tools for helping students determine how they might respond under certain conditions and then to reflect on whether those responses would be as effective as they'd like them to be. Here are a few examples of scenarios that work particularly well with students.

Case Study #1: Judd Gementle

Imagine that you're taking a seminar class in which one of your fellow students, Judd Gementle, repeatedly dominates discussions and ridicules other students, including you, for your point of view. One day you're eager to share an idea that occurred to you related to that day's discussion, but every time you try to speak, Judd keeps shutting you down with remarks that demean you and your ideas.

1. What, if anything, should you as a student do as a result of Judd's actions?
2. What would you expect the professor to do? How might you handle the situation if the professor did nothing? How might you handle the situation if the professor actually seemed to be encouraging Judd?
3. Does the setting of this scenario in a classroom affect your response? Should it have affected Judd's behavior? What aspects of the time, place, and manner of Judd's remarks and frequent interruptions are relevant here?
4. Suppose that you're having a quiet lunch one day and Judd comes up to you uninvited and continues to harangue you as he often does in class. What would an effective response be?
5. How does the issue of free speech enter into this scenario? What are the extent and limit of Judd's right of free speech? What are the extent and limit of your right of free speech?

Case Study #2: I. V. League

Suppose you're taking a course that's required for your major from Professor I. V. League. Professor League is, in your opinion, very haughty and acts in a dismissive way if students don't agree with every idea introduced in class.

At times you've been amused when watching Professor League humiliate students you regard as obnoxious and excessively opinionated. But lately the professor's wrath, for whatever reason, seems turned on you. When asked a question in class, you barely get out a few words before Professor League shouts "Wrong!" and proceeds to take apart your arguments in a manner that you find insulting. You even approached Professor League during office hours and expressed your concerns. Professor League responded, "Academic freedom means that I can conduct my classes however I see fit. You have no right to question my pedagogical methods. If you can't stand the heat, get out of the kitchen. Maybe another program is better suited to your delicate sensibilities." You explored the option of transferring to another section, but Professor League is the only person who teaches this required course. You've even considered changing your major as Dr. League suggested. Sometimes you feel so frustrated that you've considered transferring to a different school.

1. What do you believe your next step should be?
2. Imagine that you go to Dr. League's department chair to complain but are told that the chair fully support's Dr. League's claim of academic freedom. "A professor is free to choose the method of how best to teach a class," the chair tells you. "Professor League is one of our most distinguished faculty members." What do you do next?
3. At the end of the course, you receive a grade far lower than you believe you deserve based on the written assignments and tests that were returned to you. When you go to Professor League to ask about it, you're told, "Didn't you read the syllabus? It says there that class participation is forty percent of your grade. Your class participation was terrible." Do you have any further recourse?

Case Study #3: Colonel O'Trooth

As a requirement for one of your classes, you're attending a public lecture by Colonel O'Trooth who's recently published a new book about the military. Since reading this book was an assignment in the course, you're already familiar with the colonel's ideas, and you find them utterly objectionable. Colonel O'Trooth's views about the use of military force in both foreign and domestic conflicts is exactly the opposite of your own, and the colonel is known to be a prickly, argumentative figure. Even so, you're hoping that you might have an opportunity to challenge a few of the speaker's premises during the question-and-answer session. But Colonel O'Trooth is so strident in support of ideas that you find morally objectionable that you can barely remain in your seat. In instance after instance, the colonel declares as "facts" statements that you know are utterly false. Even when a statement is technically correct, Colonel O'Trooth presents it in such a misleading context that it becomes tantamount to a lie. A fellow student who shares your views happens to be sitting next to you. After a particularly outrageous remark by Colonel O'Trooth, the student says to you, "We shouldn't have to listen to this garbage. No one should. Let's start shouting and drive Colonel O'Trooth from the stage."

1. How do you respond to the other student's suggestion?
2. Suppose that the audience did begin shouting Colonel O'Trooth down, and the lecture broke up in chaos. Would you feel that the outcome was justified?
3. Imagine that a student comes up to you after the speech and says, "I'm so outraged! I loved Colonel O'Trooth's book and agree with its premise one hundred percent. What happened at the speech doesn't represent me and my views. I'm tired of being silenced by extremists!" How do you respond?
4. Imagine that another student comes up to you after the speech and says, "Well, *that* was a fiasco. I didn't agree with a single word Colonel O'Trooth said, but I still wanted to hear what the colonel had to say. What happened in there just makes students look closed-minded and plays into the hands of those who want to dismiss our point of view. It makes us *all* look bad." How do you respond?
5. In the scenario and the questions, you received no indication of Colonel O'Trooth's gender. What gender did you envision while you were reading this case study? Why do you believe that was so?

Case Study #4: Evan Jellist

Every day on your way to class, you have to pass by Evan Jellist, a local religious fanatic who harangues all the students who pass by. It is Mr. Jellist's belief that anyone who doesn't believe exactly what he does is doomed to eternal damnation and probably should be imprisoned (or worse) now "to avoid contaminating the planet with evil and heretical ideas." Ordinarily you'd just ignore Evan Jellist, but he espouses beliefs that are diametrically opposed to your own on every subject. Even worse, he's taken to singling you out as you pass by, somehow intuiting your opposition to his views, and shouting insulting remarks at you.

1. What do you do?
2. Is Evan Jellist merely engaging in his right of free speech? Is it appropriate that he do so on your college campus? Is it appropriate that he harangue individual students?

3. Suppose that Evan Jellist didn't espouse beliefs contrary to your own but actually agreed with you on every issue. Would you still feel the same way about the appropriateness of his haranguing individual students?
4. Suppose you saw another student in a heated argument with Evan Jellist as you were coming out of your class. (Assume that you don't have anywhere to go immediately.) What are you likely to do?

Case Study #5: Rigid as a Board

Imagine that the governing board of your college or university has just imposed a policy to which you are strongly opposed. You believe that this new policy will not only be detrimental to your own education but also harm the reputation of the school as a whole. You decide to attend the next board meeting as an observer. At one point during the meeting, there is an opportunity for guests and observers to pose questions to the board. You wait your turn and then ask a question that reveals your opposition to the new policy. The presiding officer of the board cuts you off. "That's enough! We don't have to hear any more. The board makes the policies at this school, not the students. We can't have the inmates running the asylum. Now sit down like a good student and listen while we do our jobs. You might learn something and, from what I just heard, you could stand to learn a thing or two."

1. What are you likely to do next?
2. Was the presiding officer acting within the rights of the board to speak to you in this manner? If so, what justification does he or she have? If not, what policy or guideline did he or she violate?
3. Was the presiding officer merely exercising his or her right of free speech? Were you?
4. Suppose that others in the audience believe that you were treated poorly and decide to prevent the board from continuing until you receive an apology. From that moment on, any time a board member speaks, there's a loud uproar from the audience and the speaker is drowned out. Would you join in with this shouting?
5. The precise areas that fall within the domain of the governing board can vary somewhat from institution to institution. Where would you go to find out precisely what falls within the board's purview at your school?

Discussing These Cases with Students

While it may be true that questions arising from scenarios like those presented here have no right or wrong answers, it also seems to be true that not all answers are *equally* right or wrong. Some answers are likely to be more effective that others in deescalating a situation and achieving a desired goal. In discussing these cases with students, the person in charge of the exercise might ask such questions as these:

1. What would you like to see as the outcome of this situation? In other words, what do you hope to attain here?
2. Is the approach you said you would take likely to achieve that outcome?
3. What other approaches might a person take in a situation like this one?
4. Is one of the other approaches more likely to achieve your goal better than the approach you said you would take?
5. If we grouped all the possible approaches you've identified into two categories—skillful approaches and unskillful approaches—which possibilities would you assign to each category?

Questions like these help students see the scenario in a larger context. The discussion can then guide them from thinking solely in terms of what feels right at the moment to considering as well as what may be beneficial to themselves and others in the long term. It also provides an opportunity for the discussion leader to mention other resources that are available to students, such as the institution's grade appeal policy, an ombuds office (if one exists), the student life staff, and so on.

EXERCISES FOR FACULTY, STAFF, AND ADMINISTRATION

Students are not the only members of a campus community that can benefit from the study of hypothetical scenarios. Faculty members can be asked to explore case studies that deal with increasingly difficult challenges.

- A student in one of your courses will not stop talking while you are presenting new material.
- A student in one of your courses makes disparaging remarks about you while you are presenting new material.
- A student in one of your courses loudly challenges you while you are presenting new material and doesn't refrain from this behavior even after you have *asked the student politely* to do so.
- A student in one of your courses loudly challenges you while you are presenting new material and doesn't refrain from this behavior even after you have *insisted* that the student do so.

- A student in one of your courses loudly challenges you while you are presenting new material and doesn't refrain from this behavior even after you have insisted that the student *leave the classroom*.
- A student in one of your courses loudly challenges you and aggressively moves toward you during class.
- The student who challenged you in one of your courses is waiting for you by your office door when you return from class.
- The student who challenged you in one of your courses is waiting for you by your car at the end of the day.
- The parent of the student who challenged you in one of your courses shows up at your office, is very angry and abusive, and refuses to leave after being asked to do so.

You can also provide other gradations to this series based on the nature of your institution or the discipline taught by the faculty member. For example, you might consider additional possibilities for professors who teach in a lab with dangerous chemicals or music professors who often teach students one-on-one behind closed doors. The scenarios can also be modified for use with members of the staff or administration by describing the student as coming into the participant's office or by substituting a member of the community for the student if the participant works directly with external stakeholders.

One particularly complex and challenging scenario that the authors have developed deals with a hypothetical university and the issues that can arise from opening facilities to outside speakers. This scenario works particularly well at an extended retreat where small groups of six to eight people work out their own solutions and then compare them with the responses of other groups. The scenario is as follows.

The Case of Slippery Slope University

Slippery Slope University (SSU) is a public institution whose motto is "Silencing the voice of one silences the voices of everyone." True to this philosophy, SSU conducted a survey several years ago to see if its students were being adequately exposed to the full range of political views. To its surprise, SSU discovers that a full 73 percent of its faculty self-identified as liberal or progressive, 15 percent self-identified as nonpolitical, while only 12 percent self-identified as conservative.

Concerned about providing students with exposure to all sides of an issue, in August of the current academic year, SSU adopted a new policy: Any group of any political philosophy could book its facilities for public presentations at a modest cost. Care would also be taken to invite representatives of those viewpoints to speak to classes. During the first month of this new policy, the results were very positive. A full spectrum of political ideas was being shared, and student attendance at public events was high. The Department of Political Science encouraged students in its courses to attend those events and invited the speakers to present their perspectives in several classes.

In September, the first hints of potential problems began to occur. Several groups with extremist views—some reactionary conservative, others radically liberal—booked SSU facilities for presentations. The extremism of these positions concerned a number of people within the SSU community, but the argument was made that "the best antidote to extremist speech is more free speech, not less of it." Besides, First Amendment rights were regarded as of paramount importance, and many people cited the SSU motto, "Silencing the voice of one silences the voices of everyone." The Department of Political Science still encouraged students in its courses to attend the presentations and invited the speakers to take part in their classes.

When October arrived, an unforeseen situation arose. The university was approached by a number of external groups advocating for what many at the school regarded as alarming economic policies. One group wanted to eliminate taxation and tariffs entirely. "What someone earns should be that person's sole possession. No one else has the right to say how people should spend their money, not even the government." Another group wanted to impose a flat tax of 90 percent on all income and of 100 percent on all possessions over $1 billion.

In return, healthcare, medication, education at all levels, and a wide range of public services would be free for everyone, and care would be taken that each resident of the country (not merely citizens and permanent residents but all residents) would receive a spending allowance no less than $50,000 a year and no more than $500,000 a year. Any income above half a million dollars would revert to the federal government.

"Those policies are all impractical!" many people at SSU protested. Nevertheless, it was argued that economic issues are sometimes impossible to separate from political issues and that students could use what they learned in the professors' classes to point out why such extremist policies wouldn't work. "Besides, we've already decided that students should be exposed to the full range of political issues. Remember: First Amendment rights are of paramount importance and 'Silencing the voice of one silences the voices of everyone.'" After some debate, therefore, the economic groups were allowed to make presentations across campus, and faculty members in political science, economics, and business encouraged their students to attend and gave the speakers access to their classes.

Then, in November, a new concern arose. The university was approached by several religious groups that supported the concept of intelligent design and opposed the teaching of the theory of evolution. These groups argued that the earth was only several thousand years old, not several billion, and that all animals and human beings were created as part of a divine plan. Many in the SSU community argued that these presentations were not appropriate at a public university. Nevertheless, the case was also made that First Amendment rights were of paramount importance and that "Silencing the voice of one silences the voices of everyone."

To the outrage of the external groups, the November presentations were only sparsely attended, and no professor invited them to co-teach their classes. When they complained to SSU that, contrary to its mission, the university was tacitly suppressing their views, administrators claimed that was not the case; posters for the events were just as plentiful as those for the political and economic presentations, and the events were advertised in exactly the same way. "Ah, but your political science faculty, economists, and business faculty encouraged students to attend the other events," representatives of the religious groups claimed. "Did your biologists, physicists, and geologists do the same for ours? And why were we never invited to present our views in the classroom"

Faculty members from the natural sciences areas were contacted and confirmed that they hadn't encouraged students to attend the "young earth" presentations or those on intelligent design and hadn't invited the religious groups to speak to their classes. "Why not?" the representatives of those groups asked. "Don't you believe that First Amendment rights have paramount importance and that 'Silencing the voice of one silences the voices of everyone'?"

For the sake of good community relations, therefore, faculty members in biology, physics, and geology encouraged their students to attend these religious presentations and invited the speakers to defend their views in class. "After all," the professors said, "students can use what they learned in our classes to point out why such bizarre notions are false." Many speakers took advantage of attending the professors' classes, and attendance at the public events in December was once again high.

In January a group of Wiccans and New Age religionists asked the university for use of its facilities to make presentations on the effectiveness of magic. Administrators at SSU were reluctant to agree but they figured they'd been down this road before. After much debate, they concluded that First Amendment rights were of paramount importance and "Silencing the voice of one silences the voices of everyone." "Excellent!" the Wiccans and New Age religionists replied. "As a matter of consistency, we'll expect that faculty members in chemistry, nursing, and medicine will encourage their students to attend and that'll we'll have an opportunity to speak in their courses."

Administrators at SSU gulped at this notion, but argued that, for the sake of consistency, they'd better encourage faculty members in chemistry, nursing, and medicine to follow the example of their colleagues in other disciplines. Because resolving this issue had taken so long, the administrators were still debating how best to encourage attendance at these events in February when a request came from a group calling itself the Postmodern Counterfactual Society with a philosophy that "Nothing is real. Nothing is true. Nothing is a fact."

The Society wanted to use SSU's facilities for a series of presentations on why $2 + 2$ equal 6, 95, 111, and 234.8 simultaneously, every circle is actually a cube, and any number divided by zero equals five. As the administrators' eyes widened, the representatives of the Postmodern Counterfactual Society continued, "We know you'll approve our request since First Amendment rights have paramount importance and 'Silencing the voice of one silences the voices of everyone.' Oh, and we also assume that all your mathematicians and logicians will encourage their students to attend our presentation and that we'll be invited to speak in their courses. By the way, I'm invisible."

1. Do colleges and universities have an obligation to expose their students to diverse views?
   a. If they do, in which disciplinary areas should this occur? If you would exclude certain disciplinary areas, why would you do so?
   b. If they don't, why not?
2. Suppose someone argued, "But political and economic issues are matters of opinion. Mathematic and geologic issues are matters of fact." How would you respond to a professor of political science or economics who said, "But I can demonstrate to you, with evidence, why conservative [or liberal] political and economic policies work and why policies from the opposite perspective don't."
3. Did SSU make a mistake in insisting that First Amendment rights were of paramount importance and that "Silencing the voice of one silences the voices of everyone"?
   a. If it made a mistake, was the principle wrong or was the way in which SSU implemented that principle wrong?
   b. If the way in which SSU implemented the principle was wrong, was it wrong from the very beginning or did it go wrong in one of the months during the academic year? (If the latter, in which month did matters go wrong?)
4. If SSU didn't make a mistake in insisting that First Amendment rights were of paramount importance and that "Silencing the voice of one

silences the voices of everyone," are you troubled by anything at all that occurred at this institution?

5. Suppose someone argued, "First Amendment rights are indeed of paramount importance. You can't start abridging them because, if you do, it's a slippery slope; there will be no way of stopping."

   a. How do you imagine that person would respond if you asked, "So, I presume that this same argument applies to the Second Amendment as well?"

   b. How do you imagine that person would respond if you asked, "So, I presume that this same argument applies to the Sixteenth Amendment (which establishes federal income taxes) as well?"

6. How might members of the faculty and members of the institution's governing board (or state legislature) view some of the issues presented in this case differently?

7. The Higher Education Act of the State of Illinois (110 ILCS 305/100) includes the following language:

   > Black History course[:] . . . [T]he University shall offer a course studying the events of Black History, including the history of the African slave trade, slavery in America, and the vestiges of slavery in this country. These events shall include not only the contributions made by individual African-Americans in government and in the arts, humanities, and sciences to the economic, cultural, and political development of the United States and Africa, but also the socio-economic struggle that African-Americans experienced collectively in striving to achieve fair and equal treatment under the laws of this nation. The taking of this course shall constitute an affirmation by students of their commitment to respect the dignity of all races and peoples and to forever eschew every form of discrimination in their lives and careers. (110 ILCS 520/85, 2019)

   a. Do you believe that legislatures should mandate aspects of the curriculum in this way?

   b. What conclusions, if any, do you draw from the provision's title "Black History course" even though it uses the term "Black History" only once and refers to "African-Americans" twice? Are the terms "Black" and "African-American" synonymous? Should they be?

   c. Suppose a state adopted the following law for its flagship university.

Reaganomics course: The University shall offer a course studying the developing of Reaganomics and other policies advocated by the fortieth president of the United States, including proposals to increase defense spending while cutting taxes, the lifting of the Soviet grain embargo, the dismissal of thirteen thousand striking air traffic controllers, and the signing of the Gramm-Rudman deficit reduction bill. These topics shall include not only actions taken by Ronald Reagan himself but also the contributions made by others in his administration in government and in the arts, humanities, and sciences to the economic, cultural, and political development of the United States, as well as the socioeconomic struggle that political and economic conservatives experienced collectively in striving to achieve fair and equal treatment under the laws of this nation. The taking of this course shall constitute an affirmation by students of their commitment to respect the dignity of all peoples and to forever eschew every form of liberalism in their lives and careers.

Do you believe that legislatures should mandate aspects of the curriculum in this way? If so, why? If not, what (if anything) makes the Reaganomics course different from Illinois's mandated black history course?

The Case of Slippery Slope University forces members of the faculty, staff, and administration to explore several key issues. Is a college or university indeed a place where any opinion may be expressed, or does higher education always "filter" speech according to such criteria as professional standards and peer review? Do we approach the matter of opinion differently in the sciences from how we approach opinion in the humanities, fine arts, and social sciences? If we do treat opinion differently based on the discipline in which that opinion is being expressed, *should* we do so? If a respected scientist dismisses a certain concept as "crackpot," how is that different from when a respected economist dismisses a certain concept as "crackpot"? When professors invite external speakers into classes (which, after all, have had their syllabi approved through peer review and the credentials of the instructor validated as meeting acceptable standards), what responsibility does the instructor of record have for what the guest speaker says?

In addition, this case study compels participants to think through when (if ever) institutional representations should intervene in matters of free speech and when they shouldn't. It provides opportunities for those involved in the exercise to review such concepts as prior restraint, the heckler's veto, and (most obviously) the slippery slope fallacy.

Both within and outside of higher education, people will often reject certain decisions or policies as "the first step down a slippery slope," "opening a can of worms," or "setting a very bad precedent." But as the students in logic courses have been taught for years, the slippery slope argument is actually a fallacy. The argument leaps immediately from a current action to a worst-case scenario without recognizing that there are multiple intervening steps where crucial decisions have to be made along the way.

Those who engage in slippery slope arguments should be reminded that there are plenty of cases in which the outcome that some would regard as a logical, ultimate consequence never occurred. Granting women the right to vote in England in 1918 and the United States in 1920 did not lead to children and babies receiving the right to vote. The abolition of prohibition in 1933 did not lead to heroin being sold at grocery stores. Allowing your children to decide what movie to watch doesn't mean they get to decide whether to go to school the next day. Providing funding for one part-time faculty member to attend one highly relevant conference doesn't mean the institution is then required to send everyone to any conference anywhere.

People sometimes forget the complex procedures that are involved in many decision-making scenarios, particularly in higher education. Simply because A happened, it is simply not the case that Z is "inevitable." They also forget that organizations learn from their mistakes and can change course before they "slide down" the proverbial "slippery slope." Prohibition is an excellent example of the ability of entities to self-correct. To many people, it sounded like a good idea in 1920. It turned out to be counterproductive in many ways, so in 1933 the United States changed course.

Colleges and universities act in a similar way all the time. They try out new courses and programs and, if those don't work out for any reason, they stop offering them. In much the same way, if a certain free speech policy is adopted with the best of intentions but has consequences that are unintended and undesirable, those policies can always be modified or new policies can be written. All too often a great deal of attention is paid to free *speech* while the arguments surrounding it overlook the fact that people also have free *will*.

Another type of hypothetical case study that works very well for members of the faculty, staff, and administration is role play. Role plays help people immerse themselves in possible scenarios and to envision how they and others might react when faced with various challenges. The role play explored here involves a controversy over a monument on a college campus, but you could adapt it to any issue that might arise in your institution or program.

A Monumental Challenge

For more than a century the administration building at Mistaken Priorities College has looked out onto a seventy-five foot monument topped by a statue of Corporal Beauregard Punishment, a Civil War veteran who was instrumental in the college's founding. Corporal Punishment had made his fortune by expanding his family's cotton plantation, where even his admirers acknowledge that he was a "rather hard master," before serving the Confederacy and, after the war, becoming an unreconstructed defender of white supremacy.

Over the years there have been periodic discussions of removing the corporal's monument, but recently these discussions have been far more rancorous. Both supporters of the monument and those who want it removed have been involved in noisy demonstrations, scuffles with the opposition, and activities that have repeatedly interrupted classes and public events on campus.

The governing board of Mistaken Priorities College has agreed to take up the question of whether the statue should be removed. But the board also wants the issue finally put to rest. As a result, it has voted that whatever decision has been made at today's board meeting will be in effect for the next twenty-five years. If the vote is to keep the statue, the board won't consider the matter again during that period. If the vote is to remove the statue, the board won't consider restoring it for the same length of time.

Not unexpectedly, that decision has caused yet another loud demonstration on campus. People on both sides of the issue have forced their way into the board meeting, and you are participating in what happens next. You will play one of the following roles.

- The chair of the governing board, who is (nominally) in charge of the meeting and who simply wants to deescalate the matter and allow the vote to be taken
- A member of the governing board who adamantly opposes the statue's removal
- A member of the governing board who is strongly in favor of removing the statue
- A faculty member who adamantly opposes the statue's removal
- A faculty member who is strongly in favor of removing the statue
- A student who adamantly opposes the statue's removal
- A student who is strongly in favor of removing the statue
- The college president who is caught in the middle and who merely wants this issue to go away
- The provost who desperately wants not to offend any of the parties in the room

For the purpose of this exercise, each of the groups that is divided (i.e., the governing board, the faculty, and the students) should have roughly the same number of people on both sides of the issue. There is no need, however, for each group to be of equal size. The role play often works best when the students outnumber the faculty who in turn outnumber the board.

Those who want the monument to remain should voice (loudly) their belief that removing the monument means turning the back on history, that Corporal Punishment did many good things (like found the college) in addition to his more nefarious acts, and that, once the precedent is set for removing one monument, there will be nothing to stop others from wanting to remove the statues of Thomas Jefferson, Mother Theresa, and Martin Luther King, Jr., which are also on campus.

Those who want to remove the monument should voice (equally loudly) their belief that the monument runs counter to the college's commitment to diversity, that the monument has served as a lightning rod for white supremacist groups in the area, and that the monument brings negative publicity to the college on a regular basis.

Both sides of the issue should also feel free to add their own arguments, even if those arguments seem irrational or ill-advised. They should do their best to counter the other side by passion, righteous indignation, and sheer volume. To avoid having the exercise become no more than a shouting match, however, the person acting as chair of the governing board is authorized to demand periodically that everyone else be silent and to recognize as an authorized speaker someone of his or her choice.

The goal of the board chair, president, and provost should be to maintain order as much as possible. The goal of the faculty and students will be to demand that their ideas be heard. The goal of the governing board will be to encourage whichever side each individual member is assigned to agree with and to try to silence or overrule the other side.

This exercise takes fifteen minutes to conduct. If it is allowed to run beyond that length of time, arguments and actions usually begin to repeat themselves, and the exercise becomes less productive. At the close of the exercise, all participants should engage in a discussion of what (if anything) went right at the hypothetical meeting of the board, which problems seemed to be the most difficult to address, and what each group could have done to make its argument in a more effective manner.

In the book *Start Talking* (2008), Kay Landis of the University of Alaska Anchorage discusses her institution's Difficult Dialogues Initiative, which will be explored in the next chapter. As part of this initiative, Landis encourages members of the university community to use role plays as a way of exploring controversial issues and provides advice on how to construct your own role play. According to Landis, the development of a good role play has four steps.

1. *Scripting*. An actual or hypotheticals incident is selected, and the number of participants necessary to create the scenario is set.
2. *Casting*. The roles are assigned to participants with the person in charge acting as director to make sure that the exercise runs smoothly.
3. *Staging*. The role play is conducted, possibly several times if different ways of resolving the issue need to be explored or if the participants wish to try out different roles.

4. *Critiquing.* The group discusses the lessons learned from the exercise (Landis, 2008, 124).

As Landis notes, role playing—particularly where the participants go through the same scenario several times—is one of the most effective ways in which difficult scenarios can be explored because this activity brings the theoretical down to the practical level in a realistic way.

[Role playing] works even though nobody has a definitive answer. It works because it's a practice. Through repetition, the sting goes out; through alternate responses, you have a real chance of discovering a strategy that will work for you; through practice, you have a better chance of responding more productively the next time you find yourself in a similar situation. (Landis, 2008, 124)

LEARNING FROM SCENARIO ACTIVITIES

But what happens if a similar situation never arises? Have you merely wasted your time engaging in a hypothetical mind game with no real value? The answer to these questions is that scenario planning is not just about envisioning actual scenarios but also adopting a mindset that might be called *scenario thinking.*

The very reason why institutions engage in scenario thinking is that the future is highly unpredictable. If, in the course of scenario planning, they happen to envision an actual scenario that later arises, the result is excellent. They've now had an opportunity to plan for an eventuality they would otherwise have missed. But scenario planning doesn't lose its value if one happens not to envision a future situation that actually occurs. Simply by developing the flexibility to respond nimbly to changing circumstances is an important outcome of this activity.

Scenario planning is a valuable tool in making a college or university what Peter Senge, the director of the Center for Organizational Learning at the MIT Sloan School of Management, calls a *learning organization.* According to Senge, a learning organization is an institution that continually reinvents itself because it engages in systems thinking (understanding how each part of the organization affects and is affected by each other part), dynamic mental models (the assumptions the organization makes about itself and the world), and team learning (the insight contributed by each member of the group to create a level of understanding not possible for any one individual) (Senge, 2006).

Even institutions that have a mission rooted in learning, colleges and universities don't always rise to the level of becoming learning organizations. The statements "But we've always done it this way" and "We tried that, but it didn't work" are at least as common in the academic world as they are in other organizational cultures. This type of institutional "tunnel vision" can be highly destructive when there is campus incivility or a challenge to free speech because the customary way of responding is not necessarily the best way of responding.

By engaging widely in scenario planning, faculty, staff, and students develop the understanding that challenges often have not one cause but many and so require an innovative and flexible response. They become used to thinking about the wide range of factors that shape the higher education environment and how the most obvious factor driving a situation may not be the *ultimate* factor driving a situation. They see the process of cause and effect not as a single row of dominoes where each effect has one and only one cause but as a complex web of interrelated causes and effects.

Consider the benefits of the following scenario exercise. A mixed group of faculty members, administrators, staff members, and students are asked the following questions.

1. Imagine that you receive a message consisting solely of the following: "A riot is taking place right now on your campus." What else, if anything, would you feel you needed to know in order to respond appropriately?
2. Would you wait until you received all that information before responding, or would you respond immediately? If you believe an effective response would require at least part of the information you specified, which piece of information do you regard as absolutely vital?
3. Once you received the information you regarded as absolutely vital, what are the first three things you would do? In what order would you do them?
4. How might your response need to be different if you later learned that the message "A riot is taking place right now on your campus" referred to each of the following scenarios?
   a. A loud but nondestructive student protest against a new campus policy.
   b. A loud but nondestructive student protest against a matter of national interest (such as a war, the government's response to a pandemic, or a frightening new report about climate change)?
   c. A loud but nondestructive protest consisting largely or solely of people unaffiliated with your institution in any way.
   d. A student protest that damages a highly controversial monument.

e. A protest by nonstudent community members that damages a highly controversial monument.

f. A student protest that results in damage to a campus building.

g. A protest by nonstudent community members that results in damage to a campus building.

h. A student protest that results in a campus building being set on fire.

i. A protest by nonstudent community members that results in a campus building being set on fire.

j. An invasion of campus by an extremist group armed with weapons.

k. An individual with mental challenges who is shouting insults at passersby, some of whom also shout insults in return.

While conducting this exercise, one or more participants might respond, "None of these different possibilities changes what I'd do. I'd call campus security [or the police] in each case." That response can lead to a discussion about whether involving law enforcement in a situation where someone with mental challenges who is acting irrationally is always the best approach. "What other options do we have at our disposal?" you might ask. "Are any of those other options more likely to bring us to a satisfactory outcome than immediately involving law enforcement?"

Participants in such an exercise will then be able to respond more effectively in the event that one of the scenarios mentioned here actually occurs. But even if none of those scenarios do occur, they're more likely to reflect on what exactly they need to know and how to determine the full range of possible responses to *any* challenging scenario that arises.

CONCLUSION

Scenario planning has a wide range of uses in higher education. As a component of strategic planning, it can reduce the likelihood that strategies will fail because the future they're based on doesn't emerge. As a pedagogical technique, it can teach students to examine the effects of certain policies or ideas by tracing their effects in different environments. And in the effort to balance free speech with civility, it can enable people to view issues from different perspectives and to respond more skillfully to various contingencies when they do occur.

Probably the most important contribution scenario planning can make to a college or university, however, is to promote scenario thinking and enable the school to become an example of Peter Senge's learning organization. Scenario planning doesn't assume that an institution will "get it right" the first time, but it does decrease the likelihood that it will "get things wrong."

It fosters creativity by compelling participants to envision different versions of the future. It fosters empathy by compelling participants to see matters as others might see them. And it fosters dialogue by bringing different constituencies together to ask various kinds of "What if?" questions.

This ability to respond in flexible and creative ways is important in higher education because of what are known as "black swan events." The term *black swan* has come to be familiar from the statistician Nassim Taleb's 2007 book *The Black Swan: The Impact of the Highly Improbable*. It refers to events that are so rare they couldn't have been predicted but, once they occur, have dramatic (usually negative) results.

Administrators can develop strategic plans for all kinds of scenarios they *do* foresee, even if changing circumstances mean that not all of those events will actually occur. Scenario planning adds to that practice the preparation for both a wider range of foreseeable events and the skill to respond more quickly and effectively to the "black swans" that otherwise might overwhelm the campus.

KEY POINTS IN THIS CHAPTER

- When crises occur on campus, they are often either the result of events no one could foresee or events that someone did foresee but others disregarded as unlikely.
- Scenario planning both prepares for a wider range of possible futures than does strategic planning and helps an institution become a learning organization that can respond more nimbly and effectively to unexpected events that occur.
- Scenario exercises for students helps them predict how they might respond in various situations and to adjust their responses if they seem likely to be ineffective or counterproductive.
- Scenario exercises for members of the faculty, staff, and administration can serve as a valuable corrective to the assumption that they already know how they'll react to events that challenge free speech or civility on campus and equips them with a better toolkit of possible responses.
- Scenario exercises for all members of the institutional community can help stakeholders see issues from the perspectives of other constituencies and thus understand why they might respond to opportunities and challenges differently.

QUESTIONS FOR REFLECTION

1. If you were to conduct a scenario exercise at your institution, which three challenging situations do you believe are most likely to occur in the near future and thus should be discussed?
2. What is one event that, although highly unlikely, would make a good scenario exercise at your institution because if it ever *did* occur, people would otherwise be caught unprepared?
3. Of the scenario exercises presented in this chapter, which do you believe would be most useful for members of your campus community to conduct?
4. Which stakeholder groups at your institution do you believe could best benefit from a scenario exercise?

REFERENCES

110 ILCS 520/85: Black History Course. (2019.) http://www.ilga.gov/legislation/ilcs/documents/011005200K85.htm.

Landis, K. (ed.) (2008). *Start talking: A handbook for engaging difficult dialogues in higher education*. Anchorage: University of Alaska Anchorage and Alaska Pacific University.

Senge, P. M. (2006). *The fifth discipline*. New York: Random House Business.

Seymour, M. and Moore, M. (2000). *Effective crisis management: Worldwide principles and practice*. London: Thomson Learning.

Taleb, N. N. (2007). *The black swan: The impact of the highly improbable*. New York: Random House.

RESOURCES

Buller, J. L., and Reeves, D. M. (2018). *The five cultures of academic development*. Washington, DC: Case.

Chermack, T. J. (2011). *Scenario planning in organizations: How to create, use, and assess scenarios*. San Francisco: Berrett-Koehler.

Lindgren, M. (2014). *Scenario planning: The link between future and strategy*. New York: Palgrave Macmillan.

Oluo, I. (2020). *So you want to talk about race*. New York: Seal.

Chapter Five

Free Speech and Civility across the Curriculum

The strategies that were discussed in Chapter 3 were valuable ways of increasing *knowledge* about issues related to free speech and campus civility at a college or university. Some institutions, however, have found that just knowing about case law and the history of academic freedom, collegiality, and similar issues doesn't go far enough. They also want students and faculty members to *experience*—and, if possible, to *immerse themselves* in—the process of balancing the right of free speech with the goal of expanding civil discourse.

This approach can be likened to the "writing across the curriculum" (WAC) approach to composition that has become increasingly common on American college campuses since the mid-1970s. The basic idea of WAC is that progress in effective written communication shouldn't occur in English courses alone. There are different styles of writing, such as lab reports and business proposals, that have their own format and style, and the types of written expression that are appropriate in one academic field aren't always appropriate in another.

Colleges and universities often develop WAC courses for other reasons as well.

- Many college students assume that writing has only one purpose: to communicate information from one person to another. But writing has many more dimensions than that. *Writing to learn* is the process by which scholars work out ideas in a written format that help them see connections and make discoveries they might otherwise have missed. *Writing for self-understanding* allows people to process their emotions and deal with experiences that they may find difficult to discuss orally. *Writing to create*

provides students with an outlet for innovation and self-expression that allows them to grow as expressive and imaginative people.
- Many college students tend to compartmentalize knowledge. They see biological understanding as relevant only in biology classes, musical knowledge as relevant only in music classes, and psychological insight as relevant only in psychology classes. College professors will sometimes hear the complaint, "Why are you correcting my grammar and style? This isn't an English course." By reinforcing the idea that written communication is important across the disciplines—and hence throughout most aspects of life—WAC courses break down this compartmentalization and see connections among academic approaches they might otherwise have missed.
- Many college students reach the postsecondary level with insufficient writing skills or poor communication habits. At some high schools, the writing of term papers has become uncommon, and college students often view a five- or ten-page paper as a significant challenge. Increased class sizes and the expectation that teachers focus on material addressed in their systems' standardized tests have reduced the amount of time that can be devoted to writing in class. Writing is a skill that tends to become easier and better the more one engages in it. So the incorporation of *any* form of writing into a WAC course can help students improve in *all* forms of writing.

Incorporating a focus on free speech and civility across the curriculum has many of these same goals. It reinforces for students that free speech and civility have more than one purpose and are relevant in more than one area. Free speech is not simply about expressing one's beliefs. It is about listening as well as talking, providing evidence as well as opinion. By confining discussion of these topics only to a first-year seminar or a political science course, schools miss a valuable opportunity to illustrate how issues of free speech and civility cut across nearly every dimension of life.

Moreover, like writing, free speech and civility are skills that become better and easier with practice. It's one thing to understand *intellectually* that others are entitled to their own opinions; it's another thing entirely to act on that understanding when those opinions are being shouted at your face. By providing students (and faculty members as well) with repeated practice in achieving a desirable balance between free speech and campus civility, schools help the theoretical become more practical. They increase the emotional intelligence of their community members, not merely their academic understanding of complex issues.

A number of colleges and universities have adopted the approach of teaching free speech and civility across the curriculum with a mixed record of success. Examining their experience with this approach can help institutions develop strategies that best suit their own mission, goals, and individual needs.

WIDENER UNIVERSITY: THE COMMON GROUND INITIATIVE

Widener University, a multicampus, private university headquartered in Chester, Pennsylvania, inaugurated what it calls its Common Ground (CG) Initiative to provide its students with a shared background in how to engage with others about controversial topics in a civil and constructive manner. As the program says in its mission statement,

> We create opportunities for students to discuss differences in open and respectful ways, preparing them for personal success and to become active participants in a thriving democracy. The Common Ground Initiative engages students in challenging yet civil conversations that teach them to:
> * Lead with integrity
> * Listen actively and openly
> * Have the courage to voice their beliefs
> * Respect different perspectives and opinions
> * Seek to understand before reacting . . .
>
> Widener's Common Ground Initiative is a national model for colleges and universities to engage students, faculty, and staff in civil dialogue that teaches them to listen and bring together people with different perspectives (Common Ground, n.d.).

What launched the CG Initiative wasn't any specific event on Widener's campus but rather a perception by the university's administration that the national mood in the United States had changed. As Widener's president, Julie Wollman, explains,

> I felt it was important to launch Common Ground after the election of 2016 because it was very clear that we were not doing a good job of listening to each other in our country. A university should be a place where we learn to listen and to respond effectively to ideas that seem misguided or feel uncomfortable to us. What better place was there than a university to model challenging conversations, respectful listening to diverse viewpoints and robust but respectful debate? My thought was that we have a responsibility to prepare our students and to support our faculty and staff in being active participants in a thriving democracy and that we had the power to model something our country really needed. Because some of what we have to listen and respond to may seem inaccurate or even repugnant, this work is linked in some ways to free speech issues,

particularly as they may play out on campuses and in classrooms. (Wollman, personal communication, July 2, 2020)

The way in which the CG Initiative would meet these goals was through a combination of coursework and co-curricular activities. CG sponsors political debates, group discussions, and political engagement groups. And because support for the initiative from the very top of the institution is important, President Wollman makes a point of holding small-group discussions related to the theme of the program.

Whenever possible, campus events are encouraged to have breakout sessions dealing with free speech and civility. Multicultural campus organizations are asked to incorporate this theme into their activities. Panels are held where speakers present ideas from diverse perspectives in a respectful and constructive manner. President Wollman describes the evolution of these activities as follows.

> Our kickoff [for the initiative] was at the National Constitution Center (NCC) with our law school dean, Rod Smolla, a constitutional law expert, and the CEO of the NCC, Jeff Rosen, also a lawyer and expert in constitutional law. And it took off from there with presentations and workshops regionally and nationally and regular CG conversations on campus which are well-attended by faculty, staff and students and are co-facilitated by me and our Chief Diversity Office, Michelle Meekins-Davis. I have also been asked to facilitate CG conversations in classes and with other groups on campus. (Wollman, personal communication, July 2, 2020)

A major goal of the CG Initiative is to help students develop practical skills they can use both in their professions and elsewhere in their lives after they graduate. These skills include emphasizing passion not perspective (i.e., even people who propose different approaches often care equally about solving the problem), causing improvement not winning (i.e., just because one party in a discussion succeeds, it doesn't mean that other parties have to lose), and focusing on empathy not confrontation (i.e., differences of opinion give people an opportunity to view matters in new ways, not simply to insist that their own perspectives are the only ones that are acceptable).

CG has also evolved over time as new issues and social challenges have arisen. Dean Smolla reports that

> the murder of George Floyd [in 2020] changed the arc of our common ground discussions, leading to town meetings with hundreds of law students, faculty, and administrators. What emerged was an understanding that we cannot achieve common ground without accepting how often our past grounds were not common, but separate, scarred by systemic racism and implicit bias, and how as

a society we must reckon with the past in order to forge a more just future. (Smolla, private communication, July 4, 2020)

The initiative thus carried historical lessons taught in the classroom into public meetings about contemporary topics. Rather than being locked into a specific curricular format, CG has been designed to change in such a way as to remain timely even as the events that led to its creation fade as memories.

Widener University has encouraged other colleges and universities to use the CG Initiative as a blueprint for their own free speech projects. In 2019, President Wollman and Dean Smolla returned to the NCC to conduct a workshop on finding common ground within the context of free speech. Their hope is that other colleges and universities might follow Widener's lead in making this issue an institutional priority.

THE DIFFICULT DIALOGUES INITIATIVE

About a decade before CG was launched at Widener, two other schools— the University of Alaska at Anchorage and Alaska Pacific University—engaged in a joint effort between the two universities to address several goals simultaneously: to improve student learning, to provide faculty members with the skills they need to deal with challenges that occur in their classrooms, to create a community that was more inclusive of minority voices, and to foster a safer, more civil environment in which differences of opinions could be shared. As those who led the initiative have declared,

> [As faculty members, we] are content experts. We know our subjects; we can write about them, talk about them, research them, defend them. But most of us have spent very little time learning how to teach and virtually none preparing ourselves to deal effectively with controversy. Ask us what to do about the biblical literalist who challenges our teaching of evolution, the insensitive student who makes a racial slur, the conservative who complains about our liberal bias, the aggressive student in the front row who dominates the conversation, or the quiet one in the back who never says a word, and suddenly the room goes silent. (Landis, 2008, ii)

Conceived, therefore, largely as a faculty development opportunity, the Difficult Dialogue Initiative includes a number of elements. First, there is a Faculty Fellowship Program designed to create a cohort of well-trained college professors who would immerse themselves in proven techniques for engaging in civil exchanges of views and serve as a role model for others. Second, there is a weeklong Faculty Intensive in which the fellows explore such topics as codes of conduct, white privilege, theological arguments at public institutions, and taking the lessons of the program "out into the world."

Third, the "Book of the Year" program at both universities is used as a platform for addressing controversial issues. Among the books selected for this program were Yasmina Khadra's *The Swallows of Kabul* (2002), Anne Fadiman's *The Spirit Catches You and You Fall Down* (2007), and T. C. Boyle's *The Tortilla Curtain* (1995). Whenever possible, authors were invited to campus for public presentations. Although other universities encountered challenges when adopting this strategy (e.g., Georgia Southern University as mentioned in Chapter 1), the two universities involved in the Difficult Dialogue Initiative took special care to prepare faculty members for this activity.

Promotional materials were prepared, workshops were held for faculty members to exchange pedagogical strategies, and discussions of the books were held during fall orientation activities. As the organizers of the initiative discovered, "It can take up to a year of advance planning to launch a successful book program" (Landis, 2008, vi). Unlike other schools that inaugurated "Book of the Year" programs as bonding experiences for first-year students, the goal of the Alaska program was "to provoke serious discussions at all levels throughout the curriculum" (Landis, 2008, vii).

To measure the impact of the Difficult Dialogue Initiative, ongoing assessment was conducted in three key areas: the faculty members' perception of their skills and level of comfort in dealing with controversial issues or difficult students; the effect the program had on the universities' learning environment in such areas as inclusivity, the encouragement of students to speak their minds, and comfort in dealing with such issues as race, religion, sexual orientation, and politics; and preservation of academic freedom, rights, and responsibilities.

As part of the initiative, faculty members were exposed to a number of teaching techniques that proved useful in addressing controversial topics. Among the techniques explored were formal debates, impromptu responses to quotes that present only one side of a controversial issue, and the following strategies.

- Respecting the Silence: not immediately speaking when students are asked a difficult question but allowing them to process the question and respond when they feel ready.
- The Circle of Objects: an examination of artifacts that have important symbolic significance in the cultures of students represented in the class.
- Cocktail Party: a role-playing exercise in which a controversial or offensive topic is raised and students are encouraged to mingle and deal with the topic civilly and respectfully as they might at a formal cocktail party.

- The Five-Minute Rule: when a marginalized perspective is raised, the first five minutes are set aside only for those who speak constructively or positively about the perspective before criticism and challenges are permitted; this technique is a way of ensuring that loud, critical voices don't drown out positive voices (Landis, 2008, 256).

As the success of the Difficult Dialogues Initiative grew, it was supplemented by other programs such as Stop Talking, where the ways of teaching and learning developed by indigenous peoples were explored and applied to the setting of a college or university, and Toxic Friday, where participants learned to deal with intimidation, bullying, and other uncivil behaviors.

FLORIDA ATLANTIC UNIVERSITY: THE AGORA PROJECT

If the CG Initiative was largely student focused (with some faculty elements) and the Difficult Dialogues Initiative was largely faculty focused (with some student elements), there have also been attempts to engage all of an institution's stakeholder groups equally. Like many creative ideas, the Agora Project at Florida Atlantic University (FAU) arose out of a problem: tensions had arisen between the faculty and upper administration; rancor was affecting the ability of the faculty senate and other major committees from making as much progress as they would have liked; disagreements that should have been kept on the level of ideas were increasingly becoming personal.

To address these issues, a group of faculty members and administrators decided that a positive type of intervention was needed. As William Trapani, the associate professor who became director of the initiative described it,

> Our original intent in developing The Agora Project was to recover a sense of the relevance of the academy to public culture and civic enterprises, to reclaim—as it were—the idea that universities are singular and irreplaceable institutions in our collective lives. In order for universities to play their essential role as a catalyst for the vitalizing work they do, there was a need to resuscitate the decorum and wonder of the university as an idea/ideal. That goal in turn meant talking about civility in very particular ways. For example, colleges and universities need to focus their discussions about civility less on manners and more on respect for the ideas and figure of the Other. They also need to reclaim a nuanced sense of academic freedom, trying to keep joined the freedom to explore and discuss potentially controversial notions while still honoring the various responsibilities that come with that affordance. (Trapani, personal communication, May 20, 2020)

The initiative was named after the *agora*, the public space in ancient Greek city-states that served many of the same functions that a *forum* did in later Roman cities. The idea was that, like a Greek agora, the new initiative would provide a civic space where ideas could be exchanged in a manner that was constructive and forward-looking. In the words of the program's website,

> The agora was the vibrant center of the city; a place where political issues of the day were debated, goods were marketed, scientific theories were exchanged, crowds were entertained by musicians or theatrical productions, and the community came together to socialize and share their lives with one another. (The FAU Agora Project, 2017)

This ambitious goal was pursued in a number of ways.

- The Speakers' Corner, inspired by London's Hyde Park Corner, was an open forum where anyone who wished could share views, discuss ideas, and exercise his or her freedom of speech.
- Presentations on civility and civic engagement were made to more than six thousand students, faculty members, administrators, staff members, and other segments of the university community.
- Brochures, flyers, posters, banners, and additional promotional materials dealing with free speech and civility were distributed.
- A website was developed from which users could download resources for classroom use or personal edification on such topics as academic freedom; civility; civic engagement; the media; and the university's Peace, Justice, and Human Rights Initiative.
- A campus climate survey was conducted.
- Workshops were held on how to engage civilly in difficult dialogues.
- Students were trained as "Agora Ambassadors" so that they could provide peer-to-peer discussions about free speech and civility with fellow students. For a semester of service, the Agora Ambassadors received an honorarium and a letter of commendation they could use for professional purposes.
- A faculty research initiative was funded.
- A Civility Module was created with materials in Microsoft PowerPoint and Word so that faculty members could incorporate these materials directly into their courses.
- A large number of topical forums, public debates, speaking contests, and open discussions were held.

In addition to these activities, a Civility Statement was developed that professors could drop directly into their syllabi:

Civility Statement
    Civility is genuine respect and regard for others: politeness, consideration, tact, good manners, graciousness, cordiality, affability, amiability, and courteousness. Civility enhances academic freedom and integrity and is a prerequisite to the free exchange of ideas and knowledge in the learning community. Our community consists of students, faculty, staff, alumni, and campus visitors. Community members affect each other's well-being and have a shared interest in creating and sustaining an environment where all community members and their points of view are valued and respected. (Trapani, personal communication, May 21, 2020)

The Agora Project was highly successful. But in addition to providing examples of activities that other institutions can borrow, FAU's Agora Project also offers a cautionary tale. Its success largely led to its demise. Once the campus atmosphere had improved, the attention of many of those on campus began to focus on other, seemingly more pressing issues, and the initial enthusiasm that led to the launching of the initiative waned.

In early 2016, the academic affairs contribution to the funding of the Agora Project ended. The Division of Student Affairs offered to move the initiative entirely onto their budget, but the director felt that doing so would have gone counter to the program's original intent. The goal of the Agora Project had been to provide a resource for the *entire* university community, not the students alone and certainly not as a program that focused on student conduct.

With the emergence of a new strategic plan, many of the program's aims were folded into the university's existing Peace, Justice, and Human Rights Initiative, and the Agora Project was largely shuttered by the spring of 2016. The lesson, therefore, is that colleges and universities hoping to replicate some of the successes of the Agora Project should first reflect on why they are doing so. If the goal is merely to solve an immediate problem of incivility or noncollegiality, then launching a major new initiative only to let it fade away in two or three years is likely to increase the very level of cynicism and distrust that the initiative was created to reduce.

BUILDING AN ACROSS-THE-CURRICULUM PROGRAM

Across-the-curriculum programs are useful because they build community by embracing the very concept of community. They reinforce the idea that free speech isn't the province of an individual discipline like journalism or political science alone, and civility isn't an ideal that should be limited to the student conduct code. Instead they illustrate how free speech and civility can help to augment one another by serving as fundamental principles of higher education.

If your school is considering the development of its own program of this sort, there are a number of lessons to be learned from schools that have already tried to implement such an initiative.

- The most effective across-the-curriculum programs are those that aren't even limited to the curriculum. They should include co-curricular activities like academic clubs and guest lectures, as well as extracurricular activities like athletics and social organizations. The idea should be that a concern for free speech and civility shouldn't stop when people leave the classroom.
- As a way of achieving this goal, the planning committee for the program shouldn't consist solely of faculty members. Student life representatives, coaches, campus security officers, students, governing board members, and other constituencies have an important perspective on the topic of free speech and civility, and they should have representatives on any planning committee.
- An across-the-curriculum program is most likely to survive and flourish if it is closely tied with a school's mission, values, and strategic plan. New concerns arise continually at a college or university. Today's concern may be free speech and civility, but tomorrow's may be sustainability in a time of reduced budgets or improving graduation rates. If the program you develop isn't integral to your institution's DNA, it's likely to be forgotten as soon as the next "hot topic" emerges on campus.
- In a similar way, the program shouldn't be created merely as a technique for solving a current problem. Many schools only consider civility initiatives when there has been a notable rise in incivility or address free speech only when there has been a well-publicized problem with censorship. The best time to develop an across-the-curriculum program is when neither free speech nor civility are being challenged in any significant way. The program is most likely to be successful when it seeks to preserve assets that already exist, not serve as a bandage to heal a wound that is in danger of festering.
- Your program is most likely to succeed if it has support from the top. Is this initiative something that is likely to receive the blessing of your president and provost? Would they speak publicly about it? Would they allocate funding for it? Even though high-level support is valuable for the sustainability of an across-the-curriculum program, it's also true that upper-level

administrators should not be the *only* voices heard when the initiative is being discussed. Students, other faculty members, and even board members (if possible) should be featured on websites and in publication talking about the benefits of the program. What do they feel that they themselves have gained by the attention your program has drawn to the issues of free speech and campus civility?

CONCLUSION

Programs that promote free speech and campus civility achieve their goals in two ways. First, the content of the program itself alerts all stakeholders of the college or university to the importance of a civil but open exchange of ideas. Second, the symbolism of how the program is designed underscores these goals. It isn't just a faculty program or a student program. It isn't just for new students or for upper division students. It isn't just for journalists, political scientists, or English majors. It's for *everyone*.

The very process of designing an across-the-curriculum program in free speech and civility becomes an exercise in the focus of the program. People will have different ideas about what the program should include and which activities should be given the greatest priority. There's likely even to be opposition to the very idea of such a program when so many other priorities are competing for scarce resources. Different divisions of the institution will want to "own" the program.

Working through these issues requires candor, diplomacy, and mutual respect, the hallmarks of what a program in free speech and civility should represent. Your program is likely to be shaped by early stages in its planning. If those discussions are transparent and cordial, your program will have greater credibility than if it's viewed as designed by a small group seeking to advance its own political agenda.

In Chapter 2 it was noted that Theodore Hesburgh, when he was president of the University of Notre Dame, regarded the free, respectful, and reasoned exchange of perspectives as a fundamental feature of higher education. While you may or may not agree with the Fifteen-Minute Rule that Hesburgh developed, that ideal of teaching students not what to think but how to think and how best to advocate in favor of their principles is an ideal that can be promoted among every member of a college community through programs that promote free speech and civility across the curriculum.

KEY POINTS IN THIS CHAPTER

- Programs that address free speech and campus civility across the curriculum seek to immerse faculty, students, and administrators in this important topic, not merely teach students the facts about this topic.
- Good models for an across-the-curriculum program on free speech and campus civility already exist. Faculty members and administrators who are considering such a program should begin by examining the programs that have already been attempted or established.
- Across-the-curriculum programs can fail when strategic goals of the administration change.
- The best across-the-curriculum programs are those that derive organically from the mission and vision of an institution.

QUESTIONS FOR REFLECTION

1. If you were to design an across-the-curriculum program on free speech and campus civility, what features would you want it to have? How would you integrate curricular, co-curricular, and extracurricular programs into this initiative? If you were to create a planning group, whom would you select to serve on it?
2. Do you believe that free speech and campus civility is a high priority for your upper administration? Is it a high priority for your governing board? How would a program dealing with this issue relate to your school's mission and vision? Can you relate such a program to your school's strategic plan in a clear and meaningful way?
3. Imagine that an across-the-curriculum program on free speech and campus civility was launched at your institution but failed within five years. What do you believe might have gone wrong?

REFERENCES

Boyle, T. C. (1995). *The tortilla curtain.* New York: Viking.
Common Ground: Widener University. (n.d.). https://www.widener.edu/about/points-pride/common-ground.
Fadiman, A. (2007). *The spirit catches you and you fall down.* New York: Farrar Straus and Giroux.
The FAU Agora Project: Florida Atlantic University. (2017). http://www.fau.edu/agora/.
Khadra, Y. (2002). *The swallows of Kabul.* New York: Anchor.

Landis, K. (ed.) (2008). *Start talking: A handbook for engaging difficult dialogues in higher education.* Anchorage: University of Alaska Anchorage and Alaska Pacific University.

RESOURCES

Merculieff, L., and Roderick, L. (2013). *Stop talking: Indigenous ways of teaching and learning and difficult dialogues in higher education.* Anchorage: University of Alaska Anchorage.

Roderick, L., and Landis, K. G. (2016). *Toxic Friday: Resources for addressing faculty bullying in higher education.* Anchorage: University of Alaska Anchorage.

Wollman, J. E. (2019). Universities already protect and promote free speech. *The Philadelphia Inquirer.* https://www.inquirer.com/opinion/commentary/campus -free-speech-zones-20190315.html.

Wollman, J.E. (2018). Widener president: Finding common ground and encouraging civil debate. *Philadelphia Business Journal.* https://www.bizjournals.com/philadelphia/ news/2018/01/05/widener-president-finding-common-ground-and.html.

Chapter Six

Developing a Comprehensive Approach

As should be apparent by now, the three central strategies just presented—making concerns about free speech and civility a teachable moment, engaging in scenario planning, and addressing this issue across and even beyond the curriculum—are not mutually exclusive. Having a well-designed educational website doesn't prevent an institution from engaging in case studies and role plays, and this type of scenario examination doesn't obviate exploring free speech and civility across the curriculum. In fact, the most productive approach would be to adopt all three of these strategies simultaneously.

But how do you do that in practical terms? And once your program is established, how do you prevent it from being phased out, like Florida Atlantic's Agora Project, when new problems, priorities, and budgetary needs arise? This final chapter explores the answers to these questions and provide you with the tools you need to address challenges involving free speech and campus civility at your institution.

THE MISSION OF HIGHER EDUCATION

One of the characteristics of higher education in the late twentieth and early twenty-first centuries is the apparent fragmentation of the university. If you ask people, "What is higher education for?" you'll receive many different answers that are not always overlapping or even complementary. To some stakeholders, the purpose of higher education is abundantly clear: it's to get a job. In an interview, when discussing the reasons for going to college, the governor (and later senator) from the state of Florida Rick Scott said the following:

The way I think about it is I went to school to get an education so I can get a job. So, I think what we ought to make sure is our university system—all of our higher ed— . . . [is designed in such a way] that when you finish, you have the opportunity to go get a job. You're in a better position. So, . . . the way I would think about it is . . . "What types of jobs are there out there?" . . . Because I believe students are similar to what I was like. I wanted to be able to get an education and go get a job. And today, as you know, you end up with more debt than you did back when I was in school. So, we need to make sure that our students know the types of jobs that are going to be out there. We're offering the courses in the programs so that people can get a job. . . . [Some people struggle to find employment.] A lot of them got degrees in areas where it was difficult to get a job. (Scott, 2012)

In a clip that lasts a minute and a half, Scott mentions jobs seven times (plus two more times in tangential comments that were elided out of the quotation). His perspective is absolutely clear: the purpose of higher education is employment, and colleges and universities that don't prepare their students for employment fail in their mission; the only programs that should be offered in higher education are those that are directly vocational. Scott's antipathy for such disciplines as anthropology and psychology is well documented. (See, for example, Anderson, 2011; Harper, 2011; and O'Connor, 2011.)

Those who see the primary goal of higher education as the production of capable employees often regard college as a private good: it is the employee who benefits most from the experience, so the prospective employee should be the one who pays for it. Indicators of a successful college program are to be found in employment rates for graduates and high scores on satisfaction surveys from employers on the quality of education that their employees received. Higher education is an investment like a stock or real estate: the return on this investment should be tangible, financial, and relatively rapid. Successful people are regarded as those who do well in life.

A very different view is expressed by Fred D'Agostino, a professor of philosophy at the University of Queensland.

I want to begin with something that happened around the time I was born in the wake of the Second World War. It was a report that Harry Truman commissioned about the future of higher education in America. And here's what the conclusions of that report were. . . . "The open and enquiring mind and the habits of rigorous and disciplined investigation are the marks of free men and the sinews of a free society. . . . It is a commonplace of the democratic faith that education is indispensable to the maintenance and growth of freedom of thought, faith, enterprise, and association. Thus the social role of education in a democratic society is at once to insure equal liberty and equal opportunity to differing individuals and groups, and to enable the citizens to understand, appraise, and redirect forces, men, and events as these tend to strengthen or to weaken their liberties. The first and most essential charge upon higher education . . . (*aside*: not to get you a job) . . . is that it shall be the carrier of democratic values, ideals, and processes and [cultivate democracy's] abiding elements: Its respect for human personality, its insistence on the fullest freedom of belief and expression for all its citizens, its principle that all should participate in decisions that concern themselves, its faith in reason, and its deep obligation to promote human well-being. (D'Agostino, 2014)

The contrast with Scott's view couldn't be sharper. Not only does D'Agostino explicitly state that higher education isn't about getting jobs for its graduates, but he also quotes at length the 1947 report by the President's Commission on Higher Education (Zook, 1947), which presented the purpose of higher education as promoting the values of democracy.

Those who see the primary goal of higher education as the production of informed citizens often regard college as a public good: it is the commonweal that benefits most from each student's experience, so the public should be the entity that pays for it. Indicators of a successful college program are to be found in voter turnout, civic engagement, and the graduates' own sense that they are living rich, meaningful lives. Higher education is an investment like the purchase of a book or concert ticket: The return on this investment should be intangible, cultural, and long-term. Successful people are regarded as those who do good in life.

Universities, the proponents of this perspective believe, exist to change things, not to reinforce the status quo. As the philosopher Richard Rorty said,

One of the most important things that happened in the US in the twentieth century was that the universities became the places where movements for the relief of human suffering found privileged sanctuaries and power bases. The universities came to play a social role that they had not played in the nineteenth century. Today the American universities not only form the best system of higher education in the world, but are morally impressive institutions. (Rorty, Reuben, and Marsden, 2000)

Protest and, yes, even a certain degree of incivility can thus be regarded as appropriate instruments for playing that social role. Disruption is at times the only way in which institutionally based inequities can be addressed.

Government leaders in totalitarian countries might disagree with that perspective, but so might Rick Scott and a number of other legislators and trustees of American universities. Getting a job usually involves learning the rules and playing by them, not overturning them. On one side of the debate are those who argue that promoting social justice is the greatest moral purpose; on the other side are those like John Kasich, the former governor of

Ohio, who famously said, "I believe that jobs are our greatest moral purpose" (Kasich, 2013).

Yet even this contrast between the goal of preparing future employees and preparing future citizens doesn't exhaust all the possible answers people might provide to the question, "What is the purpose of higher education?" Some might conclude that the goal of higher education is to make people happier. Others might claim that it's purpose is to prepare people for whatever they might encounter in life. Still others might say that the goal of higher education is simply to produce well-rounded graduates or to help people lead full and rich lives. And a few dozen more possibilities could easily be added to this list. The point is that higher education is one of the few commodities available today with a purpose that neither those who provide it nor those who receive it can agree on. And that lack of agreement has a profound effect on current discussions about free speech and campus civility.

MISSION, FREE SPEECH, AND CIVILITY

If, after all, the purpose of higher education is regarded primarily as preparation for employment, then legislators, governing boards, and even some students and parents are likely to feel that, in any situation where tension arises between free speech and campus civility, civility should win out. Protests, philosophical debates, and disruption of classes aren't commonly regarded as enhancing a student's employability. In fact, a prospective employer may well take a dim view of an applicant's association with any school where students have a reputation for being "troublemakers."

If, on the other hand, the purpose of higher education is regarded primarily as preparation for being an engaged citizen, a well-rounded critical thinker, or even just someone devoted to living a full, rich, and interesting life, then campus civility may be regarded as desirable while free speech would be regarded as essential. Professors might expect the skills of critical thinking they're developing in students to be exercised both inside of and outside the classroom. A protest against injustice or poor policies may be just as educational as a lecture on value proposition in marketing, perhaps even more so.

Nevertheless, while there are at least two sides to the issue of what higher education is for, it would be wrong to assume that each side treats the other equally. Those who argue that the purpose of college is to educate the whole person don't claim that graduates *shouldn't* be prepared to succeed in a meaningful and rewarding career; they merely argue that college should be that and *more*. But those who see higher education as essentially an advanced form of job training often want to *limit* the role of college in teaching skills not directly leading to employability.

In an effort to increase the likelihood that college graduates will find jobs quickly, some people have proposed limiting the number of general education courses a student is required to take. They want to penalize those who take more than four years to complete their degrees because they switch majors or explore several intellectual interests. And they argue that funding should be redirected away from the arts, humanities, and social sciences to the STEM disciplines and fields like business administration. The result at many colleges and universities is a wholesale realignment of educational programs.

In 2018, the College Art Association (CAA) began publishing a list of institutions of higher education that had considered or actually implemented substantial reductions to programs in the arts and humanities. As of this writing, the CAA lists eighteen such schools, several of which "recanted or changed direction [from their plans to eliminate faculty jobs, institutes, courses, or programs] due to outcry from faculty and students" (CAA News Today, 2020). Ironically, several of the schools cited by CAA have mission statements that give little, if any, attention to the goal of preparing students for jobs but, like Western Kentucky University, declare their purpose to be preparing

> students of all backgrounds to be productive, engaged, and socially responsible citizen-leaders of a global society. The University provides research, service and lifelong learning opportunities for its students, faculty, and other constituents [while it] enriches the quality of life for those within its reach. (Mission, Vision, and Values, 2018)

This disconnect between what a college or university alleges it is doing and what it actually does when allocating its budget creates problems for both free speech and campus civility. Free speech can be hampered if decisions are made to eliminate the very programs that have a long history of exposing students to the messy and sometimes rancorous conflicts that arise in society over issues of values, social justice, aesthetic taste, and related issues. Campus civility can be hampered if students and members of the faculty feel that their only recourse when these decisions are made is to create what the CAA called an "outcry."

If a college or university states that its mission is to educate the whole person or prepare students to become active and engaged citizens, then it should do exactly that. By all means, prepare students to become self-supporting and employable citizens, but don't *just* do that. Prepare them also to think critically about complex issues, thrive in a highly diverse society, and contribute constructively to debates about policies and priorities. Doing so doesn't mean that *either* free speech *or* campus civility need to be sacrificed.

HOW TO BUILD A PROGRAM THAT WORKS

There are actually many things that both those who see higher education as preparing employees and those who believe higher education has a broader purpose can agree on. Both well-prepared employees and well-informed citizens need to be able to analyze and solve problems effectively, communicate well orally and in writing, use technology proficiently, adapt to changing circumstances, provide for themselves and their families, and continue learning throughout their lives. They also benefit from a high degree of cultural literacy, the ability to identify the root causes of problems, understand themselves, and appreciate the perspectives of others.

Annual studies conducted by the College Board repeatedly demonstrate that those who receive a college education are less likely to fall victim to fraudulent claims by advertisers and demagogues; more likely to engage in the activities that will prolong their lives and keep them intellectually sharp; and more actively involved in economic, cultural, and personal development. They are also *better informed as voters* and *more employable and capable of helping their communities attract additional investment and increase the tax base*. (See, for example, Ma, Pender, and Welch, 2019.) So, if you want to build a program that promotes free speech while maintaining an appropriate amount of mutual respect and civility, why not start there, with the principles people can agree on, not those that divide them?

A successful program that promotes free speech, encourages mutual understanding, and fosters civil discussions about disagreements is likely to be one based on shared goals (critical thinking, lifelong learning, evidence-based reasoning) and values (integrity, reliability, perseverance), not on definite plans for achieving those goals (gun control versus Second Amendment rights, Black Lives Matter versus All Lives Matter, Defund the Police versus law and order) or specific ways in which those values are demonstrated (invest in your own community versus invest in the world community, emphasizing faith versus emphasizing reason, protecting the economy versus protecting the environment). It will help members of the campus community understand that not everyone who disagrees with them does so out of ignorance or corruption and not everyone who agrees with them does so out of entirely pure motives.

The program is also most likely to succeed if it learns from the lessons provided and mistakes made by the other programs discussed in this book.

- Like North Carolina State University, the University of Tennessee Knoxville (Free Speech at UT, n.d.), the University of Colorado Boulder, and the University of California at Los Angeles, it will have well-designed websites that can help people understand often difficult concepts related to free speech; academic freedom; civility; collegiality; time, place, and manner restrictions; case law; and the rights and responsibilities of protesters.
- If the institution is located in the United States, it will take advantage of Constitution Day and similar opportunities to relate the legal framework protecting free speech to the role of debate in a diverse society.
- It will use scenario planning as a strategy for helping the college or university become an example of Peter Senge's learning organization and thus respond more nimbly and effectively to challenges when they arise.
- It will follow the examples of Widener University, the University of Alaska at Anchorage, Alaska Pacific University, and Florida Atlantic University by approaching the issues of free speech and civility across the curriculum, regarding these matters as not the province of the humanities and social sciences alone but as relevant to the very mission of a college or university.
- It will tie its goals closely to the school's mission statement, values, and strategic plan so as to reduce the likelihood that, like the Agora Project at Florida Atlantic, it will start to fade away when institutional priorities change.
- And it will avoid taking sides in the ongoing debate about what a college education is really for, recognizing that being able to support oneself and one's family *is* a social concern and that being a well-informed citizen adds to—it does not detract from—one's employability.

CONCLUSION

In the summer of 2020, the controversy about the nature and limits of free speech emerged once again as more than 150 public figures published an open letter in *Harper's* condemning what they perceived as a chilling effect on the open exchange of ideas by those who had become intolerant of opposing views (A Letter on Justice and Open Debate, 2020). So-called *cancel culture*—the practice of boycotting or withdrawing support from companies, organizations, and individuals who do something deemed objectionable—and retribution for statements sometimes made decades earlier were regarded as leading to an environment where people were afraid to speak their minds for fear of a backlash. Essentially, the attempt to balance free speech and campus civility had, at least in the opinion of some, moved off campus.

The cosigners of the open letter, which included authors like Margaret Atwood, J. K. Rowling, and Salman Rushdie; academics like Noam Chomsky and John McWhorter; as well as major figures in other fields, noted:

> Editors are fired for running controversial pieces; books are withdrawn for alleged inauthenticity; journalists are barred from writing on certain topics; professors are investigated for quoting works of literature in class; a researcher is fired for circulating a peer-reviewed academic study; and the heads of organizations are ousted for what are sometimes just clumsy mistakes. Whatever the arguments around each particular incident, the result has been to steadily narrow the boundaries of what can be said without the threat of reprisal. (A Letter on Justice and Open Debate, 2020)

Ironically (or perhaps predictably) this indictment of vitriolic responses to free speech prompted a number of vitriolic responses. In an article in the *Atlantic* titled "A Deeply Provincial View of Free Speech," staff writer Hannah Giorgis said, "There's something darkly comical about the fretfulness of these elite petitioners" and claimed that the

> letter tacitly conflates [President Donald Trump's] raft of anti-media practices and open disdain for the press with the signatories' own irritation at the prospect of being ratioed on Twitter. . . . Too often, the people who wax poetic about free speech from safely behind a MacBook Air somewhere on the Upper West Side have not historically faced prohibitive obstacles to advancing their ideas. (Giorgis, 2020)

In the *Guardian*, writer John Ganz remarked,

> "Cancel culture" gives intellectuals something to debate, to talk and write about at a moment when most are cooped up indoors. Even better, it also comes with its own cant vocabulary that gives writers the actual words to use; no need to struggle with the hard and often unrewarding work of articulating reality in an original way, now one can just use the ready-made terms of debate. . . . Just sign your name on a letter someone else wrote and you are part of a literary cause, engaged in a valiant struggle against the forces of darkness and ignorance. Or, if you like, you can practice the other cant, where the signees are powerful villains and craven defenders of privilege faced with overdue and righteous proletarian anger. How quickly the tedium of life and all its indignities, personal and professional, can be transformed into a moment of historic grandeur. (Ganz, 2020)

To some, "cancel culture" constitutes a disaster that "will ultimately harm the most vital causes of our time" (A Letter on Justice and Open Debate, 2020). To others, hurt feelings over a rude reaction to something one said pales in comparison to a pandemic, an economic collapse, and violence by police officers against minority citizens.

As members of the higher education community, we can debate these matters or simply argue about them and then we can have a further debate or argument about whether there's even a meaningful difference. But regardless of whether we see the role of colleges and universities as producing capable employees, well-informed citizens, or both, we have a responsibility to prepare our students for active participation in a discussion that is likely to continue affecting them long after they graduate.

In the words of constitutional scholar Alan Brownstein,

> As an educational matter, students learn to think by confronting ideas that challenge their assumptions and predispositions. From a political perspective, if faculty and students want to operate in the world outside of academic institutions, they need to be able to engage with people who hold views that are starkly contrary to their own. If universities are attempting to distinguish truth from falsehood, produce new knowledge, and assist society in resolving public policy disputes, the best way to do so is through open and robust discussion of competing arguments and analysis. Of course, exposure to some ideas may be painful and unsettling. But the cost of suppressing them interferes too much with the university's core functions. (Brownstein, 2020)

KEY POINTS IN THIS CHAPTER

- There has long been strong disagreement about what college is for. Some believe its purpose is to prepare people for jobs. Others believe that its purpose is to prepare well-rounded citizens. Other people believe that its purpose falls somewhere in between or is something else entirely.
- An institution's understanding of its mission often guides the approach it takes toward free speech and campus civility.
- A comprehensive program for promoting free speech within the context of civility on college campuses might include educational opportunities about what free speech, civility, and the right to protest really entail, scenario analysis that helps people overcome either/or thinking and enables them to become flexible and creative when challenges arise, and commitment to the principles of free speech and campus civility across the curriculum and in co-curricular or extracurricular programs.

QUESTIONS FOR REFLECTION

1. How do you define the purpose of higher education? Does your definition of this purpose have any bearing on the issues discussed in this book: free speech, campus civility, or both?
2. Do you believe that there are practical strategies for promoting free speech and campus civility that were not discussed in this book? If so, what are they?
3. Read the open letter published in *Harper's* about the chilling effect that the letter's authors believes "cancel culture" has on the principles of democracy (A Letter on Justice and Open Debate, 2020). Do you find yourself agreeing more with the authors of the letter or its detractors? Do both sides have a point? If so, can those points be reconciled in any way?

REFERENCES

Anderson, Z. (2011). Rick Scott wants to shift university funding away from some degrees. *HT Politics.* http://politics.heraldtribune.com/2011/10/10/rick-scott-wants-to-shift-university-funding-away-from-some-majors/.

Brownstein, A. (2020). Making sense of 'orthodoxy' at secular and religious colleges. *The Hill.* https://thehill.com/opinion/education/525463-making-sense-of-orthodoxy-at-secular-and-religious-colleges.

CAA News Today. (2020). Colleges facing cuts to arts and humanities programs. http://www.collegeart.org/news/2018/11/08/colleges-facing-cuts-to-arts-and-humanities/.

D'Agostino, F. (2014). Higher education is not about getting a job. https://www.youtube.com/watch?v=ybYuN8vV2Zs.

Free speech at UT. (n.d.). https://freespeech.utk.edu.

Ganz, J. (2020). Is the free speech debate raging because intellectuals feel stripped of power? *Guardian.* https://www.theguardian.com/commentisfree/2020/jul/18/free-speech-internet-power-covid19.

Giorgis, H. (2020). A deeply provincial view of free speech. *Atlantic.* https://www.theatlantic.com/culture/archive/2020/07/harpers-letter-free-speech/614080/?utm_source=feed.

Harper, J. (2011). Why Florida Gov. Rick Scott was right to slam studying anthropology. *Business Insider.* https://www.businessinsider.com/rick-scott-thinks-liberal-arts-degrees-are-not-needed-unless-you-want-to-work-for-him-2011-10.

Kasich, J. (2013). Transcript of Gov. Kasich's State of State speech. *Oklahoman.* https://oklahoman.com/article/feed/503195/transcript-of-gov-kasichs-state-of-state-speech.

A letter on justice and open debate. (2020). *Harper's.* https://harpers.org/a-letter-on-justice-and-open-debate/.

Ma, J., Pender, M., and Welch, M. (1019). *Education pays 2019: The benefits of higher education for individuals and society.* https://research.collegeboard.org/pdf/education-pays-2019-full-report.pdf.

Mission, Vision, and Values: Western Kentucky University. (2018). https://www.wku.edu/about/mission.php.

O'Connor, J. (2011). Explaining Florida Gov. Rick Scott's war on anthropology (and why anthropologists may win). *StateImpact*. https://stateimpact.npr.org/florida/2011/10/20/explaining-florida-gov-scott-war-on-anthropology-why-anthropologists-win/.

Rorty, R., Reuben, J., and Marsden, G. (2000). The moral purposes of the university: An exchange. *Hedgehog Review*. 106–19. http://www.iasc-culture.org/THR/archives/University/2.3IRortyetal.pdf.

Scott, R. (2012). Gov. Scott talks about colleges, higher education in Florida. https://www.youtube.com/watch?v=XhmhnJPau70.

Zook, G. F. (1947). *Higher education for American democracy: A report of the President's Commission on Higher Education.* Washington, DC: Government Printing Office.

RESOURCES

Buller, J. L. (2014). The two cultures of higher education in the twenty-first century and their impact on academic freedom. *AAUP Journal of Academic Freedom*, 5. http://www.aaup.org/file/Buller.pdf.

McNamara, M. (2020). "Cancel culture" is not the problem. The *Harper's* letter is. *Los Angeles Times*. https://www.latimes.com/entertainment-arts/story/2020-07-09/cancel-culture-harpers-letter.

Schuessler, J. (2020). An open letter on free expression draws a counterblast. *New York Times*. https://www.nytimes.com/2020/07/10/arts/open-letter-debate.html.

Index

About the Authors

Jeffrey L. Buller is a senior partner in ATLAS: Academic Training, Leadership, and Assessment Services. He has served in administrative positions ranging from department chair to vice president for academic affairs at four very different institutions: Loras College, Georgia Southern University, Mary Baldwin College, and Florida Atlantic University. He is the author of twenty-one other books on education leadership, a textbook for first-year college students, and a book of essays on the music dramas of Richard Wagner. Dr. Buller has also written numerous articles on Greek and Latin literature, nineteenth- and twentieth-century opera, and college administration. From 2003 through 2005, he served as the principal English-language lecturer at the International Wagner Festival in Bayreuth, Germany. More recently, he has been active as a consultant to the Ministry of Education and many universities in Saudi Arabia, where he is helping to improve academic leadership across the Kingdom.

Robert E. Cipriano is former chair and professor emeritus of the department of Recreation and Leisure Studies at Southern Connecticut State University. He has a doctorate in therapeutic recreation, with an area of concentration in college teaching. He is the author of five books, one on collegiality in higher education, one on the Special Olympics, and three books on academic leadership in higher education. He has written chapters in three additional textbooks, and has published more than 180 journal articles and manuscripts. He has been awarded more than $9 million in grants and contracts and delivered in excess of 260 presentations in the United States, Asia, Canada, and the Middle East.

Other Leadership Books
by the Authors

BY JEFFREY L. BULLER AND ROBERT E. CIPRIANO

- *A Toolkit for College Professors*
- *A Toolkit for Department Chairs*

BY JEFFREY L. BULLER

- *Evaluating Boards and Administrators: Promoting Greater Accountability in Higher Education*
- *Confronting Today's Issues: Opportunities and Challenges for School Administrators* (with Chad Prosser and Denise Spirou)
- *A Handbook for College and University Advisory Boards* (with Dianne M. Reeves)
- *Mindful Leadership: An Insight-Based Approach to College Administration*
- *Managing Time and Stress: A Guide for Academic Leaders to Accomplish What Matters*
- *The Five Cultures of Academic Development: Crossing Boundaries in Higher Education Fundraising* (with Dianne M. Reeves)
- *Authentic Academic Leadership: A Values-Based Approach to College Administration*
- *Hire the Right Faculty Member Every Time*
- *Best Practices for Faculty Search Committees: How to Review Applications and Interview Candidates*
- *World-Class Fundraising Isn't a Solo Sport: The Team Approach to Academic Fundraising* (with Dianne M. Reeves)

- *Going for the Gold: How to Become a World-Class Academic Fundraiser* (with Dianne M. Reeves)
- *The Essential Academic Dean or Provost: A Comprehensive Desk Reference*, second edition
- *Building Leadership Capacity: A Guide to Best Practices* (with Walter H. Gmelch)
- *Change Leadership in Higher Education: A Practical Guide to Academic Transformation*
- *Positive Academic Leadership: How to Stop Putting Out Fires and Start Making a Difference*
- *Best Practices in Faculty Evaluation: A Practical Guide for Academic Leaders*
- *The Essential Department Chair: A Comprehensive Desk Reference*, second edition
- *Academic Leadership Day By Day: Small Steps That Lead to Great Success*
- *The Essential College Professor: A Practical Guide to an Academic Career*

BY ROBERT E. CIPRIANO

- *Facilitating a Collegial Department in Higher Education: Strategies for Success*
- *Readings in the Special Olympics*
- *Leisure Services Preparation: A Competency Based Approach*

More about ATLAS

ATLAS: Academic Training, Leadership, and Assessment Services offers training programs, books, and materials dealing with collegiality and positive academic leadership. Its more than fifty highly interactive programs, which can be conducted either in person or as webinars, include the following:

- Introduction to Academic Leadership
- Work-Life Balance for Academic Leaders
- Shared Governance: Only a Catchphrase?
- Time Management for Academic Leaders
- Promoting Faculty and Staff Engagement
- An Introduction to Academic Fundraising
- Best Practices in Coaching and Mentoring
- Stress Management for Academic Leaders
- Conflict Management for Academic Leaders
- Best Practices in Evaluating Administrators
- Emotional Intelligence for Academic Leaders
- Best Practices in Evaluating Faculty Members
- The Introvert's Guide to Academic Leadership
- Best Practices in Evaluating Governing Boards
- Free Speech and Campus Civility: What Works?
- Effective Communication for Academic Leaders
- Best Practices in Faculty Recruitment and Hiring
- Protecting Yourself from a Toxic Work Environment
- Best Practices in Retaining Outstanding Faculty Members
- Moving Forward: Training and Development for Advisory Boards
- The Changing Role of the Department Chair: A Longitudinal Study

- We've Got to Stop Meeting Like This: Leading Meetings Effectively
- Collegiality and Teambuilding: An Intensive Study of What Works
- Thriving in a Multi-Generational Work Environment: A Workshop for Academic Leaders
- Developing Leadership Capacity: How You Can Create a Leadership Development Program at Your Institution
- Developing Resilience as an Academic Leader: How to Bounce Back When Times Are Tough
- Why Academic Leaders Must Lead Differently: Understanding the Organizational Culture of Higher Education
- Getting Organized: Taking Control of Your Schedule, Workspace, and Habits to Get More Done in Less Time with Lower Stress
- Training the Trainers: How to Give Presentations and Provide Training the ATLAS Way
- Positive Academic Leadership: How to Stop Putting Out Fires and Start Making a Difference
- Authentic Academic Leadership: A Values-Based Approach to Academic Leadership
- Mindful Academic Leadership: A Mindfulness-Based Approach to Academic Leadership
- Fostering a College University: An In-Depth Exploration of Collegiality in Higher Education
- Managing Conflict: An In-Depth Exploration of Conflict Management in Higher Education

ATLAS offers programs in half-day, full-day, and multiday formats. These programs may be provided either in person or via webinar, as you prefer.

ATLAS also offers reduced prices on leadership books and sells materials that can be used to assess your institution or program:

- The Collegiality Assessment Matrix (CAM), which allows academic programs to evaluate the collegiality and civility of their faculty members in a consistent, objective, and reliable manner
- The Self-Assessment Matrix (S-AM), which is a self-evaluation version of the CAM
- The ATLAS Campus Climate and Moral Survey
- The ATLAS Faculty and Staff Engagement Survey

In addition, the ATLAS E-Newsletter addresses a variety of issues related to academic leadership and is sent free to subscribers.

For more information, contact:

ATLAS: Academic Training, Leadership, and Assessment Services
9154 Wooden Road
Raleigh, NC 27617
800-355-6742
www.atlasleadership.com
Email: questions@atlasleadership.com

www.ingramcontent.com/pod-product-compliance
Lightning Source LLC
Chambersburg PA
CBHW020005290326
41935CB00007B/308